CO-OPERATION
OR COERCION?

CO-OPERATION OR COERCION?

BY

L. P. JACKS

◆

"To shape the whole future is not our problem; but only to shape faithfully a small part of it, according to rules already known. The general issue will, as it has always done, rest well with a Higher Intelligence than ours."—CARLYLE.

New York
E. P. DUTTON & CO., INC.

COPYRIGHT, 1938,
BY E. P. DUTTON & CO., INC.
ALL RIGHTS RESERVED
PRINTED IN U.S.A.

FIRST EDITION

CONTENTS

	PAGE
PREFACE	vii
INTRODUCTION	ix

Part I—Critical

CHAPTER		
I.	GOOD BARGAINS AND BAD	1
II.	GOOD FEELING AND BAD	7
III.	THE WRONG MODEL	19
IV.	A MISLEADING ANALOGY	29
V.	GOOD FAITH THE ONLY SECURITY FOR INTERNATIONAL COMPACTS	36
VI.	FORCE	46
VII.	THE LEAGUE AS FIDUCIARY	58
VIII.	THE FRAILTY OF ALLIANCES	62
IX.	VAIN EXPECTATIONS	71
X.	THE WAR-MACHINE	82

Part II—Constructive

XI.	THE MOST PROMISING INSTITUTION IN THE WORLD	90
XII.	FIGHTING NOT ONE OF ITS FUNCTIONS	97
XIII.	TYPE OF A GOOD INTERNATIONAL BARGAIN	103

CONTENTS

CHAPTER		PAGE
XIV.	DISARMAMENT THE PRELUDE TO CO-OPERATION	112
XV.	DISARMAMENT AND ECONOMIC CO-OPERATION LINKED TOGETHER	116
XVI.	HOW TWO GREAT NATIONS CAME TO BURY THE HATCHET	127
XVII.	AN HISTORICAL PARALLEL FROM THE UNITED STATES	134

PREFACE

THE views set forward in this volume have been consistently held by the writer, and frequently expressed in public, since the Treaty of Versailles made its appearance. His first expression of them was in an article on that treaty, under the title "Why we are disappointed," which was published in *The Hibbert Journal* for October 1919. He has only to add that he is pacifically minded but not a pacifist; a believer in the League of Nations but not in the existing Covenant.

INTRODUCTION

To wise statesmen it has always been apparent, and recent events should have made it apparent to all of us, that no sovereign state will be a willing party to any plan for keeping the peace (or indeed for anything else) which infringes its sovereignty. This rules out as impracticable many a plan which is entirely reasonable in itself, and greatly reduces the ground on which international agreement can, at present, be firmly based. That a truth so obvious should have been overlooked in framing the Covenant of the League would be inexplicable were it not for the well-known fact that statesmanship, at that moment, was not entirely in its right mind.

To draw up on paper a scheme or plan which, if acted upon, would secure the peace of the world is by no means difficult. One has only to assume that sovereign states, in their dealings one with another, are prepared to act as sensible individuals would act if faced by similar problems, and any person gifted with a little ingenuity can work out an effective peace plan in half an hour, but unfortunately of no avail, owing to the fact that sovereign states do not settle their quarrels by the rule of common sense. There lies the snag on which peace-making projects come to grief: Kant's great design for permanent peace, the Covenant of the League, and many a scheme of lesser note. In the region of international policy the acting parties to the plan are not sensible individuals, but entities of a very different complexion—to wit, sovereign states armed for the assertion of their sovereignty and willing to assert it, on occasion, to the extremity of unreason and even of cruelty.

That these armed sovereign states are not sensible individuals, nor likely to act as though they were, is sufficiently proved by the present state of the world. Were they sensible individuals, or framed on that model, they would not be arming themselves for mutual destruction and bleeding themselves white in the process. "As I watch the figures mounting up," said Mr. Neville Chamberlain, "I cannot help being impressed with the incredible folly of civilisation." (January 29th, 1937.) Very well then; in offering our peace plan to civilisation let us not forget that the civilisation to which we are offering it is incredibly foolish, and let no man be surprised if his plan is received as the foolish are wont to receive a good thing when it is offered them. On one side the common sense, the scientific perfection, the high wisdom of your plan; on the other the incredible folly of the armed sovereign states that you invite to work it. What will become of your plan under these conditions?

INTRODUCTION

Nay, more. Were the High Contracting Parties in the habit of acting sensibly, the problem the peacemaker has to solve would not exist. Consider the Covenant of the League. Here we see an incredibly foolish civilisation, overtaken by a spasm of repentance, putting itself under bonds to play the fool no more. So far, so good. But, alas, at the first crisis that calls for fulfilment, itself caused by the incredible folly of some of them, the incredible folly of the others returns in full force, the bond is broken and a situation created far worse than if the Covenant of Repentance had never been made. What folly can be more incredible than to make such a contract when you know very well that it will certainly be broken precisely at the moment when most needed? If the High Contracting Parties were sensible individuals they would not act in this manner.

There is another difficulty. While each of the High Contracting Parties is more or less aware of the incredible folly in which they are all involved together, none of them regards itself as incredibly foolish. It is to civilisation, not to the British Empire, that Mr. Chamberlain applies this language, and doubtless Herr Hitler or Signor Mussolini would each make a similar exception on behalf of his own country, which each of them regards as taking wise measures to secure itself amid the general inundation of folly. Folly everywhere, and recognised for what it is by all nations, but no nation a fool in its own eyes. How difficult, under these conditions, for the nations to agree effectively to anything of importance; how unlikely that the agreement will be kept even if made! What could warn us more clearly against expecting the High Contracting Parties to behave themselves like sensible individuals?

In studying the lives of individual human beings we observe that the more highly developed an individual becomes the more inclined he is to assert his own will and, consequently, the more difficult for others to control, and the more disinclined to tolerate their interference. This is a very great difficulty in a civilisation or a culture which aims at increasing the number of highly-developed individuals and devises its system of education for that very purpose. The difficulty would be great in a wise civilisation, to say nothing of a foolish one. It accounts for the alarm, so frequently vocal of late, caused by the tendency of the modern individual to throw off the moral restraints which his fathers, less highly developed than he, accepted contentedly. But what else are we to expect in an age which looks upon the high development of the individual as the thing most of all to be desired?

It is the same with nations. As they grow in power they become proportionately more self-assertive, more resolved to be severally masters in their own houses, more jealous of their sovereignty and consequently more difficult to control by any rule of law other than that which each chooses to impose upon itself. Especially is this so when the growth of their power takes the direction of *armed* power, and when they develop their individualities in the fighting form. The greater the armed power of any nation, and its readiness for fighting, the less its willingness to submit to any will save its own. Thus it comes to pass that all the time they are increasing their armaments they are drifting further and further away from the possibility of submitting to the rule of a common law, just as our highly-developed young men and women are becoming more and more intolerant of the moral controls imposed upon themselves by their less-developed grandfathers.

It is precisely in the matter of their armed power that sovereign states show themselves most sensitive and most intolerant of interference. Put any restraint on their use of *that* and you are interfering with their sovereignty at the very point where interference is most obnoxious; you are seeking to restrain them at the very point where they are firmly resolved to be unrestrained. Agreements to that effect are difficult enough to make, but even if made they are, of all agreements, the least likely to be kept. If sovereign states were sensible individuals they would agree at once to put these dangerous armaments of theirs, created in their folly, under proper restraint and would keep the agreement after they had made it. But, as we have seen, sensible individuals are precisely what they are not, though some of them, oddly enough, are represented by statesmen of high intelligence.

Since the beginning of this century, and especially since the close of the war, these sovereign states have developed their armed power to a degree which has no parallel in history. With every step of that process they have become deafer to the voice of reason and more incapable of acting on the principles of common sense. Never did the voice of reason speak so loudly as it does to-day, but never has it spoken to ears so deaf as when addressed to these fighting states; while as to moral appeals, if involving the least concession of sovereignty, they are thrown away as completely as if they had been addressed to the carnivora. Never was the restraint of a common law so outstandingly urgent. Never were the nations, however willing to put restraint on their neighbours, so resolutely determined to endure none of it themselves. And which more resolutely than Great Britain?

A situation sufficiently disconcerting to the peacemaker. And still more so when he contemplates the race for armaments as it is now going on, every step in which renders agreement to control them more remote, for much the same reason that a drunkard, the harder he drinks, becomes less and less inclined to take the pledge or capable of keeping it if he does. Agreement in this matter has never been near at hand; now it may be said to have passed completely out of sight.

As the nations develop their fighting individualities—and the armament race means just that*—their self-assertiveness becomes an intoxication which renders them progressively incapable of agreeing about anything. The history of non-intervention in the Spanish Civil War reveals this in a very convincing way. Here we see the general incapacity to agree developing, the moment armed forces are involved in the plan, into a positive will not to agree, the mere fact that the plan has been proposed by one nation being a sufficient reason with others for opposing it, or better still, for accepting it and immediately afterwards inventing a pretext for not carrying it out. Lord Plymouth's task has been that of tying eels into a knot.

Such are the two facts which recent experience has been teaching us to recognise and ponder; first, a growing incapacity in armed sovereign states to come to agreements involving the restraint of their arms; and, second, a growing incapacity to keep such agreements even if made

---

* "We are arming for defence" means "We are developing our power as a fighting nation."

in some rare moment when, as in 1919, disaster has brought them to the mood of repentance.

Reflecting on all this, a truth seems to emerge not without value as a guide to future action. We have observed that armed sovereign states are never so unamenable to reason, and so deaf to its appeals, as when faced by proposals to put their fighting powers under the rule of a common law. Since, then, the problem of the moment is to develop in the nations a capacity for agreement, and for keeping agreements when made, would it not be wise for the present to avoid armed force as the medium in which to seek it, and to pitch the work of reconciliation in some field more hopeful, or at least less hopeless? This may not be easy to find, and even when found, we shall still be faced by the fact that the High Contracting Parties are not sensible individuals. However willing they might be to listen to reason in the form of a good bargain, there is still the danger that the still small voice of the sensible proposal will be drowned by the unreason of armed nationalism. This danger is greatly to be feared.

Nevertheless, the record of commercial treaties, so much more creditable on the whole than the record of military treaties, seems to show that while these nations are lamentably deficient in common sense when the restraint of their armed forces is in question, they are by no means insensible to the attractions of a good bargain

INTRODUCTION

and have often shown enough common sense both to make such bargains and to keep them. In that department they do reveal a certain capacity for agreement. This should be developed as the most promising line of action now open to the peacemaker.

In the later pages of this book a proposal, having this modest aim, will be brought forward. We shall approach it by stages.

CO-OPERATION
OR COERCION?

PART I - CRITICAL

CHAPTER I

GOOD BARGAINS AND BAD

THE military or fighting alliance is now so firmly established as the orthodox method of obtaining security against the designs of aggressors that our minds may have a difficulty in thinking of any other. The League of Nations itself, as far as it aims at the prevention of war, is an alliance of that type conceived on the great scale—an armed combination of the many who would keep the peace against the one who would break it. If military alliances could be trusted to keep the peace they might be considered good bargains, though, even so, the nations would be involved in vast expenditure on armaments and find peace, so secured, a ruinous luxury. But we shall see that they cannot be trusted.

From the nature of the case these alliances cannot be other than bad bargains, and frail because they are bad. There is little profit to be had from their fulfilment. Under the conditions of modern warfare there would seem to be less than none. No matter what the cause at issue may be, "righteous" or otherwise, a bargain which exposes a nation to the destruction of its cities, and the indiscriminate slaughter of the civil population by bombing raids is likely to be a bad one. In times of tranquillity the bad side of the bargain will be obscured, but revealed immediately to one or other of the parties when a crisis arises which calls for its fulfilment. Its frailty will become apparent at the same moment. There are no two nations in the world whose love is so strong and self-renouncing that each is willing to shed its blood for the other without advantage gained. Foreign policy seems wedded, none the less, to this method of securing peace, though signs are not wanting that the thinking public, taught by recent events, has begun to distrust it. In the United States, where the avoidance of "entangling alliances" is traditional, distrust of the method dates back to the time of Washington.

This form of bargaining being so obviously bad, the question naturally arises of finding a better, that is, a method more conducive to security. It were surely wiser in the interests of peace to make no bargains at all, and to sign no covenants, than to give them a form likely to be broken in the day of performance, as all bad bargains are. Nothing has done more in recent years to poison the international atmosphere and to increase the danger of war than the repeated infraction of treaties, intended to secure the peace, on one or more of the contracting parties coming to the conclusion that the bargain, so far as they were concerned, was a bad one. The Kellogg Pact, the Locarno Treaty and the Covenant of the League all broke down in this way, with disastrous results to the prospects of the peace they were intended to secure.

"Good bargains for bad" would, therefore, be a very suitable motto for all of us in these days who desire to see the peace of the world more firmly established. That they could be found, if diligently searched for, there is not a doubt. In the economic field there exists a multitude of neglected opportunities for making good bargains between the nations from which substantial benefits would accrue to the parties, and which, for that reason, would have a far better chance of being faithfully kept than the bad military bargains hitherto the fashion. If the League of Nations could be persuaded to take that line the way would be open to the realisation of its great ideal. That is what some of us may live to see.

This, however, will not be done without a bold departure from traditional methods. So long as the mind of the League, or the minds of those who guide it, are concentrated on the military field, where the bad bargains lie, the exploration of the economic field, where the good bargains are waiting, will be inadequate and casual, and the League will remain what it now is, a great ideal linked to unworkable machinery. Many new forms of military alliance are now being talked of. Before entering on any of them, whether on the great scale of the League or the smaller scale of the regional pact, we need to consider very carefully what in general such alliances are worth as instruments for the preservation of peace. This will be done in due course.* We shall find that their value has been greatly exaggerated.

In commending economic or business partnership as a more profitable form of international co-operation than military or fighting partnership, we commend it also as more conducive to peace. A partnership between the nations on a business footing would, in our judgment, do more to prevent war and to promote peace than any partnership on a military footing that could possibly be devised. Cobden held the same view, and though other Cobdenite doctrines are not now in fashion we have never heard of this one, on which the others are based, being overthrown.† It is true that our method does not aim directly at the prevention of war, nor does it promise the immediate advent of permanent peace. But seeing that the military method, after being extensively tried for many generations, has not achieved the first of these objects and shows no signs of achieving the second, the two methods at this point may at least cry quits.

* Chapter VIII.
† For an example of its application see Chapter XVI.

A League or Partnership of Nations on a business-like footing would work for peace by indirection. It would differ from a league on a military footing in making no attempt to end war by forcible suppression, and in avoiding the use of threats. Its business would be conducted in a less quarrelsome atmosphere and its oratory pitched in a less exasperating key. It would take the way round to its objective in preference to the short cut, and would aim rather at outmanœuvring war than at crushing it. We here commend it as the more promising way to peace.

By no possibility can the two methods be combined: to combine the service of God and Mammon would be as practicable. Their nature is antagonistic; what the one did the other would promptly undo; they imply different mentalities, and in the clash between them old habit would inevitably get the better of new enlightenment, and the League return to the hopeless task, which has already preoccupied its supporters far too long, of preventing war by forcible suppression—a method analogous to the ill-starred experiment of Prohibition in the United States, but under stars still more inauspicious.

In the process of rolling sheets of metal a bulge will sometimes appear on the surface of the sheet, which now becomes valueless unless the defect be removed. How can this be done? Shall we put pressure on the bulge? Shall we hammer on it till it disappears? Those who know tell us that this is the very thing we must *not* do. If we hammer on the bulge we shall crack the sheet. No: we must hammer all round it, beginning on the edges of the sheet and presently, as we get nearer the bulge, we shall find it has vanished.

Such is the peace policy this book recommends. Our sheet is civilisation and the bulge is the danger of war. If we hammer *on* it we crack the sheet. Let us hammer *round* it.*

* I got this illustration from Sir Oliver Lodge. But I believe it was originally used, in another connection, by Herbert Spencer.

CHAPTER II

GOOD FEELING AND BAD

OF all the objects on which the peacemaker could spend his efforts the one most likely to yield the results he desires is the creation of a better state of international feeling or, as we sometimes say, of a better atmosphere.

We offer this as a more temperate version of the cry, often uttered by prophetic voices in our time as in former times, that nothing short of a radical change of mind in the nations can save our civilisation from catastrophe. Unfortunately the prophet who utters this salutary warning is unable to advance any further; and the nations who hear it, and may even believe it, are unable to respond. Human means do not exist for producing a radical change of mind, suddenly or even quickly, in nations hard-set in their habitual ways of thinking and acting. Nations, like individuals, do not change their minds (or "hearts") on being bidden to do so by wise men, not even when the wise men prove the change to be necessary. They cannot. The force of habit is here vastly stronger than the voice of reason and the consequence is that the necessity of the change, even when fully recognised, does not produce it. But the situation becomes less intractable when effort is directed to changing the atmosphere in which these hard-set "minds" are wont to operate. Human means of doing this may be found, though they certainly do not consist in mere exhortation. And there are good reasons, mainly of the psychological order, for believing that if good or better feeling could be induced in quarters where bad feeling is now dominant, a general change of "mind" in the same direction would begin to follow.—We are conscious of using vague terms, but believe them to be sufficiently intelligible without entering into elaborate definitions.

To represent bad feeling as the universal condition of inter-state relations would be a gross exaggeration. That every nation hates, fears or even mistrusts every other, and that all of them are preparing to cut each other's throats, or to prevent their own throats from being cut, is demonstrably and absurdly false. Yet the international picture is often painted by alarmists or pessimists in colours which suggest that this is the actual state of things confronting the peacemaker. If it were, the situation would be quite hopeless, and it would not be worth while to write this chapter, or any chapter, on the subject. On the other hand, if the level of international good feeling could be raised all round to that at which it now stands, say, between the British and Dutch nations (often at war in the past and still commercial rivals), we should be far indeed from the universal brotherhood of the idealists, but the present generation of peacemakers might deem their cause well launched on the way to final success, and sing their *Nunc Dimittis* accordingly.

There seems no reason in the nature of things why this should be regarded as impossible of achievement, and we could hardly do better in the interests of peace than by concentrating effort, at least for the present, on achieving it. Imagine the wholesome repercussions on the international situation if the political relations between France and Germany, to look no further, could be brought even to the modest level of mutual toleration. Why not? A sound commercial treaty between the two nations, such as Dr. Schacht is said to have had in mind, might conceivably work wonders in that direction. It would not be the first time it has led two powerful nations, which had been age-long enemies, to bury the hatchet, as we shall narrate in a subsequent chapter.*

Without abandoning the ideal of assured and universal peace, should we not do wisely, for the time being, to limit our efforts to something less ambitious, resting content if only we can lay the foundation for the next-comers to build on and get in the thin end of the wedge for the future to drive home? This would be done if international

* Chapter XVI.

feeling in the areas where it is now intolerably bad could be brought to the level of the larger areas where it is tolerably good. There is no short-cut to permanent peace. Patience is necessary.

Nowhere, indeed, is the state of feeling between nations so good that a wise policy could not make it better. The present friendship of our own country with France or with the United States* might conceivably become a firmer and more fruitful friendship than it is. But on the whole it may be said that over vast areas of the world's surface, and over large areas of Europe, the state of feeling between the nations occupying these regions is sufficiently good to make the danger of war between them extremely remote, if not to eliminate it entirely. The recent proceedings of the Pan-American Congress at Buenos Aires were, in this respect, most encouraging. The state of feeling disclosed was friendly, at least in comparison with certain phenomena in Europe, and the result was considerably to increase the area of the world's surface where the probabilities of durable peace stand high. At the same time it must be confessed that the danger-spots of the world, where bad feeling is active, have become more dangerous in recent years. But there is no reason to despair. Encouraged by such examples

---

* So long as the frontier between Canada and the United States remains unfortified we are entitled to say, without producing further evidence, that this friendship exists, however capable it may be of further improvement.

as those mentioned above, and noting the methods which have produced them, the peacemaker may hopefully return to the *ad interim* task we would here assign him—that of creating a better atmosphere where the atmosphere is now bad.

Turning to the dark spots in the picture we observe that feeling is at its worst in the relations existing between certain armed Powers in Europe or, to speak more accurately, between the groups into which they are formed, the race for armaments, which registers their mutual fears and suspicions, as these have arisen in the course of their history, being rather a race between groups than between individual nations. Here it is no exaggeration to say that the prevailing atmosphere is *poisoned*, and poisoned to such a degree and by such manifold elements that peacemaking projects, however well conceived, wither and die under their blighting influence. Here are nations with no confidence in each other's good faith; where mutual loyalty is needed there is mutual censoriousness, fomented by press campaigns; honest proposals are interpreted as sinister designs; vigilance against double-dealing is incessant all round, and more than one instance could be cited of the statesman who has risen to eminence in his own country on the strength of his success in betraying another. Mistrust, suspicion, fear, hatred and revenge are the ingredients of this witches' cauldron. Above all, the atmosphere is saturated with *lies*, often deliberately propagated. Be you who you may, and bring forward what proposals you will for appeasement and reconciliation, they will immediately be overwhelmed with objections based on the suspicion, not always groundless, that this nation or that cannot be trusted, that this statesman or the other is certain to play false. In these tainted regions the tradition of fair dealing does not exist. But there is a strong tradition of equivocation, mendacity and sharp practice.

How can these plague-spots be made wholesome? It is not surprising that many persons, impressed by the conditions we have described and by the international anarchy which results from them, look to coercion, military or economic, as the only possible answer, and propose international machinery for that purpose. But this device, it cannot be too often repeated, is obviously futile so long as nations needing coercion are parts of the machinery intended to coerce them. It would therefore be necessary from the outset to make a separation between nations "known to be loyal" (whatever that may mean) and nations suspected of disloyalty, and to entrust the operation of the machinery solely to the former, on the same principle that suspected mutineers would be excluded from a commission for the suppression of mutiny. Proposals to that effect have in fact been made.

The gravest difficulties attend them. By separating the nations into good and bad, sheep and goats, violent resentment would be aroused in the goats, and hostile relations immediately established between them and the sheep. The bare assumption by the one party that they were the sheep and the others the goats would be enough of itself to put the fat in the fire. Those who propose that certain nations, selected on the ground of their own estimate of their own righteousness, should go into partnership as world-police overlook the fact that the others are by no means willing to accept these self-appointed guardians of the peace at their own valuation. The proposal, if seriously taken, would rouse the war drums in every powerful nation not included in the partnership. It would be a warlike challenge addressed to the latter and be followed immediately by a race for armaments between the two groups, to the accompaniment of intensifying hostility between them. Among the many causes which foster bad feeling not the least exasperating is the habit some nations have of assuming self-righteous airs in the presence of the others. When they go further than this by giving themselves a commission to enforce the rule of law on the rest, or even making proposals to that effect, they are taking the surest means that could be found to provoke reprisals and inflame whatever bad blood may happen to be in circulation. If the object be to create a better atmosphere, this, clearly, is not the way. It is the way to make bad feeling worse.

This result is inevitable when projects of coercion, however formulated, are set on foot among sovereign states. A sovereign state is one which, just by reason of its sovereignty, resents coercion by other states and will not submit to it but, rather than submit, will fight to the last ditch, even against an overwhelming preponderance of strength, as the little Boer Republics fought against the mighty British Empire in the South African war. History abounds in such examples, from Thermopylæ down to our own time. Threatened with coercion the sovereign state will fight if it can; and if it cannot, by reason of weakness, bankruptcy or want of courage, there will be lasting bad blood between it and any power or group of powers that puts it under restraint. Where powerful states are concerned the result in bad feeling—and this alone is what we are now considering—is even worse. Those who talk blandly, as some have recently been talking, of Great Britain, France and the United States setting up a partnership as the armed peacekeepers of the world should ask themselves what the reaction in any one of these three nations would be if a group of other powers, say Germany, Italy and Russia, were to go into partnership for keeping *them* in order—and why should they not? And even when the coercing machinery is constructed more comprehensively, as in the Covenant of the League, it will be found impossible to make it effective without pointing it, or seeming to point it, against some particular nation suspected as likely to give trouble (Germany, for example) and immediately throwing the nation pointed at into an attitude of resentment and armed resistance. Whatever the strength at its disposal may be, the coercing authority will find, at the first attempt to put its machinery into operation, that an armed sovereign state is not to be overawed by the threat of coercion and is non-coercible *so long as it stands on its feet*. In one way only can a sovereign state be coerced—by actually overthrowing it on the battlefield and so depriving it of power to assert its sovereignty in the given circumstances. Even short of the attempt to impose sanctions, the mere discussion of the project will turn every state which believes itself pointed at into a fighting enemy of the sanctionist system and so bring into being fresh currents of bad blood.

All proposals for the creation of an international force, some of which are ingenious enough, encounter the same difficulty. Practicable as they appear, or can be made to appear, when attention is confined to the problem of creating such a force, they all collapse in presence of the fact that willingness to yield to its pressure or its threats does not exist in any sovereign state on the face of the earth, and is most conspicuously lacking in the country where most of these schemes have originated—to wit, our own.

The conclusion to which these considerations point may be simply stated. All projects of coercion, whether limited or comprehensive, economic or military, form the worst possible medium for promoting good feeling, sound understanding and lasting agreement between sovereign states. This is the medium, this the atmosphere, this the context in which animosities are most inflammable, susceptibilities most irritable, suspicions most rife, interests most conflicting, unreason most active, censoriousness most virulent, resentment most easily aroused, backslidings most certain, and betrayals most likely to occur. Let those who consider this language too strong consider the dissensions that have arisen over the attempt to use international force as a patrol to secure non-intervention in Spain, and then ask what the degree of dissension would be if the business in hand were, not mere patrolling, but actual fighting, such as that which came into prospect during the Abyssinian crisis.

This medium, then, being fatal to the growth of international good feeling, is it possible to find a better?

There are many such. In some of them, and these by no means the least promising, good

GOOD FEELING AND BAD

feeling may be promoted on non-political lines, in which the direct intervention of governments is not required. Agencies for promoting intellectual co-operation in many fields, now rendered easy by modern means of communication; the interchange of university professors and students; the fraternisation of youth fellowships; the Boy Scouts; the increase of foreign travel and the more hospitable entertainment of the stranger within the gates; international sports;* international conferences—all these operate as media where good feeling between the nations represented tends to arise spontaneously. Separate mention must be made of the movement for a common language, whether an existing language or a new one. Among the causes retarding the growth of good feeling not the least is the imperfect understanding of the nations of each other's tongues.† Certainly a League of Nations which reproduces the conditions of Babel can hardly be expected to function very smoothly.

These activities, important though they be, lie outside the purpose of the present book. Our problem is that of finding a medium, more

---

* "If all the politics of the world were left to us boxers, there would be no silly nonsense like war." (Remark of the Chief Constable of Nottingham when entertaining a team of police boxers from Germany. Reported in the *Nottingham Guardian*, Sept. 26, 1936.)

† A recent instance will be remembered when the mistranslation of a single word in one of Herr Hitler's speeches, apparently intended to be pacific, caused the speech to be construed as warlike.

promising than armed force, in which sovereign states, as such, may co-operate amicably for their mutual benefit. Later on we shall indicate where this can be found.

CHAPTER III

THE WRONG MODEL

"Is the League of Nations to reproduce the structure of the armed political state prepared for fighting and with fighting forces trained for battle, or is it to be a community of another type?" (Author's letter to *The Times*, June 26th, 1937.)

ACCORDING to an argument so often repeated that it has almost become an accepted dogma, the federation of existing states into an effective League or political Union is simply a further step in the federating process by which these states, through the fusion of warring provinces and other conflicting elements within their own borders, have separately grown to be the unities they now are. World unity, as the final result, would thus be the natural outcome of a process which is now far advanced and has already produced the great political unities known as the British Empire, the United States, Germany, Italy and many others.

Following from this, or perhaps integral to the same argument, is the belief that world unity, in the form of an effective League of Nations, would merely reproduce on the universal scale the structure now exhibited on the limited scale by every well-ordered political state armed with force for maintaining the rule of law. It would, in fact, be a political state, of the same general structure as those now in existence, but differing from them in having world-wide scope and authority and, consequently, no foreign enemies to contend with beyond its own borders.

This theory enjoys considerable popularity among peacemakers and is certainly attractive for many reasons. At all events it has the merit of simplicity. But before accepting the well-ordered political state as the one and only model for an effective League of Nations and governing our peacemaking efforts accordingly, close consideration is needed at several important points.

Though some of the political states now existing may be described as well-ordered in comparison with others that are obviously ill-ordered, in none of them is the rule of law so just and equitable as to make it a satisfactory model for world unity, for an effective League of Nations or, on a more limited scale, for the United States of Europe. Even in the best ordered among them internal strife of many kinds, due in the main to felt injustice, is frequent and dangerous. None of them has yet attained such a high degree of inner tranquillity, contentment and good feeling between the various elements of the community as to justify us in believing that the reproduction of its structure on the world scale would be other than a very risky experiment. Even the most highly civilised races are less advanced in the art of government than the praise they give their institutions seems to imply. There is much abuse of power, and in many states revolution, due to the abuse of power by constituted authority, is a constant danger. In few, if in any, is that danger wholly negligible, what is euphemistically described as maintaining the rule of law being sometimes little else than the brutal suppression of revolutionary tendencies, real or fictitious. These ugly phenomena are not to be exclusively associated with the rule of dictators. Under democracy also majorities are by no means immune to the abuse of power. Dr. Inge is not without some measure of justification when he defines that form of government as "the organised plunder of minorities."

Nowhere, moreover, has a form of political structure been evolved which would be accepted without opposition as the structure proper for the federation of the states concerned into an effective League of Nations. At the present moment fierce conflict is proceeding, and perhaps fiercer conflict impending, between the partisans of two political structures that are radically different, the democratic and the totalitarian. With the final form of the political state still indeterminate and the subject of bitter strife, is it not somewhat premature to look in that quarter for the model of world unity? Would not the quarrel between the democrats and the totalitarians have, at least, to be settled first? True, a new model might be proposed on the lines of Plato's Republic or some other Utopian speculation. But what are the prospects that even well-ordered states, with no experience in working such a model, would be able or willing to conform to it, to say nothing of the ill-ordered, which are far more numerous? These difficulties are very formidable. May it not be that the political state, no matter how conceived, is the wrong model for the community of mankind—if that is what we are hoping for and aiming at? Other models are conceivable.

We have next to note that even if the theory be accepted which represents the union of nations into an organic league as a further stage, or natural continuation, of their evolution into the political unities they now are—even on that hypothesis, the history of the unifying process, so far as it has gone, does not entitle us to hope that the further stages will be peaceably accomplished. On the contrary, if the future of that process is to resemble its past a long period must elapse before the nations are delivered from the scourge of war.

Very rarely has the growth of states followed an unbroken line of peaceable development. Its normal course has been one of repeated warfare, in which the weaker provinces have been gradually conquered by the stronger. These wars and conquests have, indeed, been finally consummated by political Acts of Union peaceably negotiated. Such Acts of Union, however, are intelligible only as the outcome of protracted conflict, in which the relative strength of the parties has been decided on the battlefield, and the dominant power of the strongest clearly established. The United Kingdom of Great Britain and Ireland is a notable case in point, and the United States of America, finally consolidated after a four years' wrestle of life and death between North and South, is another. For all these great political solidarities a heavy price in human blood, spilt on a hundred historical battlefields, has had to be paid, and by none more copiously than by the British Empire. The *Pax Britannica*, like the *Pax Romana*, is a phenomenon which the lover of peace may well contemplate with satisfaction. But if we think of it as peaceably negotiated at a Round Table and then ratified by a Treaty, Covenant or Act of Union we misconceive the process which brought it into being. It has been a process of warfare, and not of discussion alone.

The internal struggles out of which the great political unities of our day have emerged have been accompanied, moreover, by the constant necessity of presenting a united front against encroachment or attack by foreign foes, and of creating a common frontier favourably drawn for resisting their military pressure. The unification of Germany after the Franco-Prussian war of 1870 or of Italy against the threat of Austrian domination, are modern examples that will readily occur to mind. Nor does the unification of the state afford any guarantee against subsequent revolution and civil war, of which a terrible example is now being afforded in Spain—a point which advocates of world federation are somewhat disposed to overlook. World federation is one thing; permanent peace is another.

Of late it has become the fashion of certain historians to underrate the importance of war as a factor in the making of nations, and to lay the emphasis rather on the process of peaceable evolution within the social structure. As a corrective to militarist tendencies there is a good excuse for this; at the same time it is obvious enough that the growth of states would be unintelligible were no attention paid to "the decisive battles of the world." Either element may be over-emphasised, but neither is intelligible without the other. In an important sense, though not to the exclusion of other factors and other aims, political states may be defined as war-made and war-making institutions; none more conspicuously so than the British Empire. Were other evidence wanting, the present race for armaments would clearly stamp that character on

THE WRONG MODEL

every nation engaged in it. This outstanding fact must never be lost sight of when the problem arises of uniting these war-made and war-making political structures into a peaceable League of Nations, and of inducing them to renounce war as an instrument of national policy. Such a renunciation might almost be described as the cutting-off of the state's right hand. It would have to change the course of its history, and make a new start in life after the manner of a converted sinner—a change not impossible perhaps, but unlikely to follow as the result of moral appeals or to be accomplished by the simple process of giving a pledge to that effect, signing a Covenant or other summary procedure.

If, therefore, the establishment of *Pax Mundana* is to follow the analogy of *Pax Romana*, *Pax Britannica*, *Pax Americana*, or any other *Pax*, by repeating the process which has brought them into being, it would seem that a long period of intermittent war and bloodshed is in store for the world before that consummation is reached. The relations now existing between the armed states of Europe, to which we may confine attention for the moment, are certainly not more amicable than those between the kingdoms of the Heptarchy in the days when they fought for the mastery, or between England and Scotland when they wrestled at Bannockburn and Flodden Field, or between North and South in the American

Civil War. Nor are there any indications that these states have yet acquired a degree of reasonableness in their dealings one with another which would incline them to convert themselves peaceably into a band of brothers. The indications are to the contrary.

Napoleon, in his day, was under no illusion about the matter. He, like ourselves, had his dream of a United States of Europe, and with that dream in mind he led a great force into Russia, his last great obstacle on the Continent, in 1812. That force was the nearest approach to an international army the modern world has seen. His purpose was to unite Europe under the power of its conquering sword. Nothing has occurred since then to suggest that it could now be accomplished at a Round Table conference of statesmen. Arguing from the analogy of past unifications, the struggle for the mastery, as the prelude to union, has yet to be fought to an issue. Fortunately the analogy is not decisive.

The conditions under which warring factions have been appeased, private combat abolished and individuals trained to obedience under their constituted governments are widely different from those which confront us when the units to be dealt with are not unarmed individuals nor even warring factions, but armed states martially disposed, hard-set in the assertion of their sovereignty and intolerant of coercion. Nor are the methods employed by these states in enforcing the rule of law upon their own nationals always so just as to form a good model for enforcing that rule in the wider realm of interstate relations. The number of states in the world to-day where law and order can be described as justly enforced is relatively small, while those where the enforcement is unjust, violent and tyrannous is relatively great. There are millions of people living in Europe to-day who, if they were free to speak, would declare that the rule of law as they know it is an evil of the first magnitude—a fine phrase, indeed, on the lips of the moralist but a most damnable reality in their experience of it. Dictators are bad enough, but majorities, as exponents of the rule of law, are sometimes not much better.

The fact is that the rule of law has nowhere reached such a degree of perfection that it can be offered, in any of its existing forms, as an unqualified boon to the nations at large. In this country the law-enforcing methods of Judge Jeffreys are happily a thing of the past, though we have still some advance to make in the direction which has led us away from them; but they are by no means extinct in Europe as a whole, not to mention other continents. The bloody assizes so frequent under the Soviet régime, the free use of the rubber truncheon in Fascist states, the massacre at Addis Ababa, and such-like phenomena, should remind us that the rule of law as enforced in the modern world is not yet on a basis so uniformly just and benign that we can take it as a working model to be reproduced on a large scale for the control of international relations. That political states, whose enforcement of law upon their own citizens takes these high-handed forms, are fully ripe for partnership in a great enterprise of international justice is a proposition that may well be doubted.

Before proceeding further on that line ought we not to assure ourselves that the reproduction of the rule of law on the international field will conform to the best and not the worst examples of its present enforcement on the national field? And how can we gain that assurance unless by assuming that the nations which are foremost in the arts of justice will manage, somehow, to make themselves masters of the world? Tempting as that assumption may be to nations which deem themselves foremost, it is certainly not the way of peace.

CHAPTER IV

A MISLEADING ANALOGY

THE Covenant of the League, as it now stands, has the form of a contract* between sovereign states binding them, at certain points, to subordinate their individual ambitions to the common interest, the common interest being here conceived in terms of peace. This aspect of it recalls the doctrine of the Social Contract associated with the name of Rousseau. According to this doctrine the reign of peace in an ordered society has its origin in a contract between the members to submit themselves to the rule of law and to combine their forces for the restraint of the law-breaker. It is precisely such a contract, with sovereign states substituted for individual citizens as the contracting units, that we have before us in the Covenant of the League.

It is generally admitted that the doctrine of the Social Contract has no historical foundation. None the less it has the verisimilitude of a well-constructed myth. Though law and order within

---

*There has recently been a correspondence in *The Times* (September 1937) on the question whether the Covenant is or is not a contract. The fact that the signatories call themselves "the High Contracting Parties" would seem a sufficient answer.

the state are the evolutionary outcome of a long struggle against their opposites, the actual result as we see it to-day is much the same as it would be if the citizens were controlling their actions under the terms of a contract signed, sealed and delivered at a given date. This interesting but deceitful resemblance probably accounts, at least in part, for the widespread belief that sovereign states can be brought in like manner to accept the rule of international law by entering into a contract or making a treaty to that effect. But the affair, as we now begin to see, is not so simple.

To the considerations already adduced the following may be added, by way of showing that the analogy of the well-ordered state is misleading when applied to the problem of creating a system of collective security, in which the acting units are not unarmed individuals but sovereign states armed for the defence or assertion of their sovereignty.

1. Of all the burdens to which the individual citizen has been trained to submit himself in the common interest, the heaviest is the burden of taxation. He is made to pay heavily, not perhaps without murmurs, but without active resistance, for the security he enjoys; the rich man in the form of a staggering income-tax with devastating death duties in prospect, in addition to indirect taxes of many kinds which the poor man shares with him whenever he smokes a pipe of tobacco

or drinks a cup of tea. Well-ordered states are expensive institutions to those who live under the protection of their laws. A long schooling, interspersed with many castigations, has broken the citizen in to the patient bearing of this burden. The contrast is obvious. A League of Nations promising collective security to the member states, but unequipped with taxing authority over them, and with no willingness on their part to countenance its creation, would bear little resemblance to any political state now in existence.

2. Collective security in the well-ordered state implies that the citizen remits his quarrels to the jurisdiction of public law. He must "leave the government to do the fighting," if fighting there is to be done. He is not at liberty to destroy his enemy if he can, nor to threaten him with lethal weapons. Except in cases of emergency, when the arm of the law is not available to protect him, the taking of the law into his own hands is sternly forbidden, and necessarily so if the collective system is to work. The principle of collective resistance by the state is here combined with that of non-resistance by the individual, except in so far as he resists his opponent by handing him over to the law.

No approach to these conditions is visible among the sovereign states now constituting the League of Nations. The tendency is in the opposite direction. While pledged under the terms of the Covenant to combine their forces for mutual protection, they show not the slightest disposition to renounce the right of independent belligerency, but continue to arm themselves without limit, the left hand thus destroying the value of the pledge given by the right. Nothing could be more inconsistent with the conditions under which the rule of law is maintained in the political state. Until the right of independent belligerency in their own defence, with the attendant right of arming at discretion for the purpose, is surrendered, the structure of their league will fail to reproduce the structure of any one of them. What are the probabilities of their consenting to this surrender?

3. While the state protects the citizen in the enjoyment of whatever property he stands legally possessed of, it gives him no security for the maintenance of that property, at its present value or in its present form. It places no obstruction in the way of its transference to other citizens. Under a system of periodical assessments it treats the distribution of wealth as fluid, adjusting its own share according to changes that have taken place since it was last assessed. It neither forbids the poor man to increase his possessions nor confirms the rich man in perpetual possession of what is already his.

If the League of Nations is to reproduce these

conditions it will have to leave room for the liquidation of existing inequalities between rich states and poor, great states and small. It will treat the territorial divisions of the world, not as fixed but as fluid. As in a well-ordered state *la carrière ouverte aux talents* is kept open for meritorious citizens, so our League, were it similarly founded, would keep open the path of advance by which small states climb to greatness, nor would it close the path of decline for great states, grown incompetent or decadent, by obstructing the transference of their possessions to those more capable of using them well. On the other hand, were our League to stereotype the inequalities existing among its members, guaranteeing the *status quo*, as we say, it would diverge so widely from the structure of the political state that all resemblance to it would vanish.

On these grounds we feel justified in saying that a false analogy underlies the current contention that a League of sovereign states is simply a further stage, or natural development, of the evolutionary process by which they have severally grown into the unities they now are. We incline rather to the opinion that this line of evolution has now reached its term. And happily so, for its course hitherto has been one of war and bloodshed which its further continuance would certainly repeat.

It will be gathered from what has been said that hope for the future of the League of Nations, as we entertain it, lies in the possibility that the League may emerge as a new type of community having a structure different from that of the political state armed for the assertion of its sovereignty. As formed on that model, or as reproducing its structure, we regard the League as defunct, and view with apprehension any attempt to revive it in that character.

Is any other model available? Strictly speaking there is none—none that the League could copy and reproduce point by point. Nevertheless, there does exist, and has long existed, a type of community founded on a principle which, with due modifications of technique, could be transferred with beneficent results to the field of international relations, now in a state approaching anarchy. This is the Community of Mutual Insurance. The principle it embodies is that of creating a common interest out of interests otherwise confused and conflicting; in other words, the principle of the Good Bargain. As an instrument of peacemaking it has great possibilities waiting to be explored and developed. Here is an acorn, which, under favourable conditions, may grow into an oak. And what, after all, is Mutual Insurance but another name for Collective Security? We think it a better name. And for this reason: that whereas

A MISLEADING ANALOGY

Collective Security has hitherto been sought in the more provocative terms of Force, Mutual Insurance employs the less provocative term of Fund, and points to the economic field, rather than the military, as the more promising for peacemaking effort. We commend this change of terminology especially to those who base their hopes of peace on the gradual emergence of a new economic world-order.

We shall return to the consideration of this at a later stage.* Our advance is blocked by formidable obstructions, and these we must first endeavour to remove.

* Chapter XIII.

CHAPTER V

GOOD FAITH THE ONLY SECURITY FOR INTERNATIONAL COMPACTS

"Do what we will, we have no choice but, in the last resort, to depend upon the plighted word." (Sir Austen Chamberlain, in a speech which is said to have killed the Geneva Protocol in 1924.)

THE League of Nations, notwithstanding its present shattered condition, stands for the highest and most enduring of all the secular ideals which the human mind has conceived or the human will sought to realise. It stands for the solidarity of the human race, for the "Hope of the Great Community." Except as pointing in that direction, or as an approach to that distant consummation it would be a thing of little significance. However unworkable its present form may be, it will never be suffered to perish from the face of the earth. Of this we may be well assured.

The League has been defined again and again as an institution for the prevention of war. This, at some stage of its growth, though not at the first, it will certainly achieve. But only as a thing to be taken in its stride towards a far more significant and positive objective. Moreover, the prevention of war will, of itself, do nothing to achieve the end in view unless the means taken to prevent war be such as to bring the nations into a closer unity and a more abiding friendship. Unfortunately the means taken by the League for dealing with aggressors are not of the kind that promotes unity and friendship. They are of the kind which causes division and conflict, as we have seen. They must be changed.

As now constituted the League represents a great ideal linked to unworkable machinery which broke down completely at the first great crisis which called for its operation. That machinery can never be restored nor patched up into working efficiency by improvements here and there. Its failure was due to no minor defects; it was due to the radical falseness of the principle on which the machine was constructed. Nevertheless the ideal it was intended to serve is imperishable and humanity quite undefeated in the pursuit of it. The first experiment, indeed, has failed, and no wonder that it has, considering the magnitude of the problem it had to solve and the inexperience of the experimenters in schemes so vast. Its failure should teach us how not to fail next time.

In devising the next experiment there is an outstanding truth which needs to be firmly grasped at the outset, and never for a moment lost hold of at any stage in the process of construction. An international compact of some kind will be necessary. *But whatever form the compact may take, however stringently it may be worded, and whatever penalties may be assigned to infraction, the fulfilment of it will depend in the last resort on the good faith of the parties and on nothing else.*

The reason for this is obvious. The parties to the compact will themselves constitute the authority responsible for its fulfilment. There is no authority beyond themselves which could prevent them disregarding their obligations *en masse*, or penalise them for doing so. No degree of severity in the punishment or coercion of a defaulter will provide security against default unless those on whom the infliction of punitive measures devolves can be relied on to keep faith one with another in whatever crisis may call for their application. If default is possible in one of the parties, what reason have we to suppose it impossible in the remainder who bind themselves to deal with the particular defaulter in such and such a way? Failing complete reliance on their mutual good faith, the punitive provision would have no more effect than a second sieve placed inside a first. Frame the compact how you will, there is no escaping the conclusion that the good faith of the parties is the one and only security for its fulfilment. An obvious truth, but easily lost sight of by those who put their trust in machinery and become absorbed in the ingenuities of constructing it—a cast of mind by no means uncommon in these days.

Who, then, are the parties to an international compact, and how do they stand in the matter of good faith as judged by their present dispositions and past record in their dealings one with another? These questions demand the most careful consideration before embarking on the next experiment in international unity. Otherwise we may find ourselves repeating the mistake of creating machinery the working of which is beyond the good faith of which the parties committed to work it are at present capable. Who, then, are these parties?

Once more they are sovereign political states, each of them armed, and some armed to the teeth, for the defence or assertion of its sovereignty; each determined to be the arbiter of its own destiny and sole master in its own house and, if need be, to resist interference to the uttermost. Unlike the unarmed citizens of a peaceful state, who have surrendered the defence of their rights to the arm of the law, and acquired the habits of law-abidingness which that surrender demands, the parties to our international compact have never surrendered the right of independent belligerency in defence of their rights, nor acquired the habit of submission to any authority which would interfere with it. In all this the habits, traditions and moral codes governing the conduct of the parties to international compacts are on a widely different level (whether higher or lower is not here the question) from those which govern the conduct of the individual citizens who compose the population, or of the individual statesmen who sign the compact on behalf of the states they represent. The moral code of the individual citizen requires him to submit to the civil authority under which he lives and to render unto Cæsar the things which are Cæsar's. This he does habitually, as his fathers for centuries have done before him, in submitting to the coercion of the tax-collector and in countless other ways.

The sovereign states which are parties to international compacts have had no such training and acquired no such habits. They may be compared to masterless, but highly masterful, men. They acknowledge no superior power whose orders they are bound to obey and are given to boasting that they have never done so and never will, every nation having its equivalent to "Britons never, never shall be slaves," though none proclaim it more loudly than the British. As sovereign, a state may indeed be willing (if sufficiently short-sighted) to enter into a compact for exercising coercive authority over another state found guilty of misdemeanour. But it can never itself *submit* to such coercion without surrender of its sovereignty—and what sovereign state in the world to-day is willing to do that?

Should a situation arise which requires it, not to impose coercion on another but to submit to coercion itself, it will immediately realise the folly of joining in a compact which places it in that position, and will promptly retire from the compact, as Japan retired on discovering that she herself was likely to become the object of disciplinary measures. And what of our own country? Were we similarly threatened, can there be a doubt that "Britons never shall be slaves" would resound from every corner of the land?

Such being the nature of the High Contracting Parties, each determined to be master in its own house, armed for independent belligerency, and with *nemo me impune lacessit* inscribed on its banners, it seems obvious that any attempt to put these masterful entities under collective discipline, however much they may stand in need of it, is doomed to failure. Their nature as sovereign states forbids them to submit. To make such a system even theoretically complete a double pledge would be required from each of the members: first a pledge to contribute its share to the imposition of discipline and then a pledge to submit to discipline if itself found in default. This second pledge no sovereign state could give without surrender of its sovereignty. To secure the peace of the world on these terms is impossible.

That such an attempt should ever have been made would be inexplicable were it not that some of the leaders in it are wedded to the assumption that, whoever else might be forced to swallow the medicine, they themselves would never be. An arrangement based on an assumption so one-sided can hardly be expected to work very smoothly. "Whoever else may turn aggressor, yet will not I" is too reminiscent of a similar protest, made on a memorable occasion long ago, to be accepted without reserve. It has been heard of late from more quarters than one. The makers of it may be sincere, but unfortunately they have little confidence in each other's sincerity. So long as that remains in doubt it is a vain thing for any nation to protest its good intentions.

From all this important conclusions follow. Since the habit of submission to authority is non-existent among the High Contracting Parties in their relations one with another, and is flatly in conflict with the principle of sovereignty itself, there remains only one way in which a covenanted group can impose coercion on a covenant-breaking member—that of making united war upon it and forcing it to its knees. Or perhaps by threatening to do so; but only on a clear understanding that the threat, if unheeded, will be remorselessly carried into effect, and the fact well known to all concerned that force adequate for the purpose is in existence and fully prepared for warlike operations. In the words of Lord Grey of Fallodon, "those states which have power must be prepared to use all the forces they possess, economic, military or naval. Anything less than this will be of no value." Peace will thus be placed under the guardianship of war, with overwhelming force on the side of the guardian, security resting not on an intangible thing called good faith but on a tangible preponderance of fighting power.

As a mechanical contrivance nothing could seem more adequate for the purpose. As set out on a blue print its success appears to be certain. But where is the driving force to come from? As sovereign states acknowledge no authority save that which each has created for itself in its own government, and take orders from no other, whence and how is an order to be issued to which all of them or any of them will render an unquestioning obedience? From a common council of the nations? There is not a single people or government in the world to-day whose willingness to involve itself in the risks of war at the bidding of such a body could be counted on for a moment. Coming from that source a decision to make common war on an aggressor would find everyone of them asserting its right to obey or to disobey as its own judgment might direct; *and this every would-be aggressor knows full well.* Futile to plead that they are pledged under a solemn covenant to make war upon him. Futile to reproach them for bad faith. They have undertaken what they are literally unable to fulfil. They could only reply, if they replied honestly, "in a moment of dim vision we pledged ourselves to that which now, in a moment of clearer vision, we find entirely beyond our power." A humiliating confession, perhaps, but less humiliating than the keeping up of a hollow pretence.

Every sovereign state, whatever its internal constitution, democratic or otherwise, is an autocrat in its external relations with the others. The League of Nations, strictly speaking, is a League of Autocrats, each claiming to be the sole arbiter of its own destiny. That these are internally democracies, and those internally autocracies, makes no difference to the attitude in which they confront one another, the attitude, namely, of those who owe allegiance to no superior power. Nothing could be further from the truth than the conception of the League as a democratic body the individual members of which have accepted the principle of bowing to a majority vote. Least of all would that principle be accepted by any of them in the matter of making or not making war. As sovereign and autocratic that decision remains indefeasibly in the hand of each.

SECURITY FOR INTERNATIONAL COMPACTS

The education of political states in good faith and mutual loyalty is the indispensable prelude to any scheme, plan or machinery that ingenuity can devise for promoting the unity and peace of mankind. One might even name it the outstanding need of the world to-day. Such an education, however, is not to be had through the medium of military alliances, either on the great scale involving all the nations or on the small scale involving only some. Military alliances are far more likely to train the nations in the habit of breaking their bonds than in the habit of keeping them. Of all the methods that might be chosen of developing the co-operative spirit and habit, co-operative fighting, no matter in what cause or against whom directed, is positively the worst.

Were the obsession once broken which leads the nations to seek their medium of co-operation in the element of armed and fighting force, with such disastrous results as we now see, the possibilities of another and far more promising medium will begin to reveal themselves. Where they lie may be indicated by a remark recently made by a prominent member of a great commercial exchange. "On this exchange," he said, "hundreds of bargains are made every week which there is no force of law to protect. Very seldom is any one of them broken."

CHAPTER VI

FORCE

THERE is a doctrine, sometimes called "the orthodox doctrine of the League," which lays it down, as an essential proposition, that without the use of force, or at least without its presence ready for use, the rule of law in international relations, as in national, is impossible. This may be freely granted on the ground that in this world nothing can be ruled or regulated, nothing can be done or got done, without employing force of one kind or another.

And always it will be found that some measure of *physical* force is involved in the transaction and that, without it, the moral forces would be quite unable to get the moral business done or the moral action performed. The Good Samaritan used considerable physical force when he ministered to the wounded man, lifted him on to the back of his animal and safely transported him to the inn. Had he been a disembodied spirit with only moral or spiritual forces at his disposal, or a mere speaking voice proclaiming the love of one's neighbour, the wounded man would have bled to death by the roadside and thousands of edifying sermons would never have been preached. Even the preaching of the Gospel would be impossible unless the preacher used enough physical force to make himself heard, and it is unfortunate for the Gospel that this is not always done. Let the reader conceive, if he can, of a moral action, or an immoral one for the matter of that, which can get itself done without the use of physical force. Strange how the notion has got abroad, among pacifists and non-resisters, that physical force in human relations is necessary only when one is doing wrong.

When therefore we are told that the rule of law is impossible without adequate force to sustain it, and that the League must be furnished with force for that purpose, we are merely being informed of what in that general form is self-evident, and we have no exception to take. A League without force would certainly be forceless. If the apostles of this over-laboured truism would be content to state it in that form there would be no place for controversy, as there would be no need for making the statement.

Further enlightenment is clearly called for. Since force is a thing of endless varieties the question now arises—what *kind* of force is the League to be furnished with, to have at its disposal and to use if need be? That question answered, a number of others immediately follow. How is the required force to be created?

How, when created, is it to be trained, equipped and controlled? Where, if anywhere, are its headquarters to be located? Who is to be responsible for its training, cohesion, morale and efficiency? By whom and how is it to be paid for? As these and other related questions are pressed, the self-evident proposition with which we started becomes increasingly questionable and finally absurd.

Dean Matthews in *The Root of the Matter* (Cassell) answers our main question as follows: "We must remove the temptation to resort to the brutal decision of war by having a collective force so formidable, so certain in action, that even a madman would hesitate to challenge it." Let us examine this statement.

From the general description it is clearly physical force, however mingled with moral force or directed by it, that Dean Matthews has here in mind. So far, so good: as we have already seen, nothing can be done, either constructively or destructively, collectively or individually, without the employment of physical force. But physical force has endless ways of operating, some gentle, humane and beneficent, others violent, cruel and diabolical. Enough if we name two of them. Physical force may take the form of *pressure*, as when a policeman pushes the crowd a little further back on the pavement; or it may take the form of *blows*, as when he begins laying about him with his truncheon and cracking skulls. Which of the two forms has Dean Matthews in mind for his collective force? Either or both?

The language employed makes it clear that blows are not excluded. The force, we are told, must be so formidable that even a madman would hesitate to challenge it. This it can hardly be unless the madman foresees that he will get badly hurt, or possibly killed, if he persists in his madness. The collective force, therefore, must be prepared to use violence, and to use it in ways that put the fear of God into the madman, not to strike merely but to strike hard enough to hurt him and kill him if need be. A force, then, that can rain blows, crack skulls and cut throats—the latter plainly indicated when the force is described as "the sword", Hobbes quoted to the effect that "Covenants without the sword are empty words," and Christian men informed by their spiritual guides that "the sword" may be drawn in a righteous cause. A fighting and killing force, trained to fight and to kill, and not afraid of madmen who have had a similar training. A force of warriors inspired by a courage and ardour for battle not inferior to that of any madman, egoistic maniac or reckless looter who may threaten to give trouble. Would anything less than this be formidable enough to satisfy the orthodox doctrine, as expounded by Dean Matthews, or to deter a Mussolini or a Hitler if inclined to play the madman's part?

It is a fatal consequence of the race for armaments that, with the nations armed as they now are, a collective force sufficient to restrain particular madmen would have to be enormous in size and armed with the deadliest weapons available, not merely bigger than the madman's but more terrible. If a particular madman has three million trained fighting men behind him the collective force which is to overawe and paralyse him must have at least four. If his three millions are armed with machine guns, tanks, submarines and bombing aeroplanes, the four must be armed with the same weapons, and equally trained in their use. Futile to threaten him with a mob of raw recruits. Futile to arm them with policemen's truncheons or even with swords "drawn in a righteous cause." Futile to confront him with "an army of lions commanded by asses." The strategists of our collective force and its commanders in the field must be at least as bold and competent as his in the art of war. If he happens to be a military genius—a gift which mad conquistadors sometimes possess—while the collective force is under the command of an incompetent general, the four millions, in spite of all the moral forces behind them, will have little chance against so terrible an antagonist.

We pass on to the second condition laid down by Dean Matthews for the collective force—certainty in action. To ensure this many things will be necessary. (1) Since our force is a collection of units contributed by many nations, we must be sure of its cohesion in any crisis that may arise; the risk of dissension or mutiny between the component parts must be completely eliminated. (2) It must be in a state of constant readiness to take action in any quarter where its services may be required, with plans prepared for dealing with likely danger-points. (3) It must keep its powder dry, never be caught napping, and exercise a ceaseless vigilance. (4) A well-organised Intelligence Department with a Secret Service must be ready to give warning of any plots that may be hatching against the common peace. (5) There must be no divided counsels, no waiting on the results of protracted discussions, no time wasted in getting up steam or in sewing the buttons on the warriors' tunics. (6) Supplies, munitions, transport, communications must be thoroughly prepared: they cannot be improvised at the last moment. Such is the minimum of what will be necessary if our Force is to be "certain in action."

Nor is it enough that it be collective; it must be *collected*, or capable of being swiftly collected. Arrangements for its mobilisation must be complete. It will never do if the component units are engaged in garrison duties at the ends of the earth, or in other operations under their respective governments, at the moment when they are needed for meeting the "madman"* on the battlefield. Their international service must be a whole-time employment, so that no question can arise of this navy or of that air force being wanted at the critical moment for service in another field. In correspondence with this, the allegiance of each unit, British, French, German or other, must be given entire and without reservation to the authority in control of the collective force. Were its allegiance divided between the country from which it came and the League of Nations under whose orders it was acting, it would obviously be of no value to the common cause and disqualified from taking part in any quarrel in which the country contributing it was the offender. From the Commander-in-Chief to the humblest private in the ranks, our Force would need to be composed of single-minded internationalists acknowledging no authority and obeying no orders save those of the League.

For the maintenance of a force powerful enough to overwhelm any of the existing armaments that might conceivably be used for lawless aggression the cost would hardly be less than £300,000,000 per annum. By whom is that cost to be borne? How is it to be distributed? Were the League of

* The terms "madman", "reckless looter", "egoistic maniac", when used to denote an aggressor, are misleading and merely obscure the realities of the situation. Morally mad the aggressor may well be, but as an opponent to be met in battle it would be the height of folly to treat him as either mad, reckless or egoistic.

Nations empowered to tax the member states to the required extent, and the member states willing to be taxed by the League, the answer would be simple enough. Unfurnished with power to tax, the League would be in the position of having on its hands a great fighting force but with no authority to raise the funds required for its maintenance and with no certain means of doing so. The position is unthinkable. Were the raising of this enormous sum left to the goodwill of the covenanting states, subject to changes of public opinion and to vicissitudes in their financial and political conditions, the arrangement would hardly be worth the paper on which it was written. No fighting force could either be created or maintained unless the authority under whose orders it was to act had equal authority to raise the funds needed for its creation and maintenance. What effective fighting force has ever existed under any other conditions?

We now see what kind of an institution the League of Nations would be if furnished with the force demanded by the orthodox doctrine. It would be a *fighting* institution, the last word in power politics, disposing of a fighting force greater than any aggressor, conqueror or "madman" is likely to bring into the field, and efficient for its purpose only on these terms.

The enormous difficulties involved in such a project are wont to be obscured by the loose and inexact terminology employed by its advocates. A favourite euphemism is "the sword," a term so remote from the realities of modern warfare that we may dismiss it without further consideration as at best romance and at worst nonsense. More useful as camouflage for the issue, but hardly less remote from the reality of it, is the term "international police." On this it might be enough to comment that, as aggressors do not employ police for their deeds of aggression, so police will be utterly useless for the purpose of restraining them, unless it takes the form of armies, navies and air forces more than equal to theirs in striking power.

Even if "police" be retained as a pardonable equivocation, we must still remind ourselves that "police" activities are by no means uniformly humane in their mode of operation. Broadly speaking, they are of two kinds: a kind which protects and a kind which persecutes. A distinguished German Professor (now an exile) recently explained the difference as follows: "In England, when you see a policeman on the street, he makes you feel safe; in Germany, when we see a policeman, he makes us feel unsafe." Which kind do our police-enthusiasts propose to employ for guarding the rule of law—the kind which makes the nations feel safe or that which makes them feel unsafe? This leads to a most important consideration.

FORCE

Let us, if we can, imagine all the above difficulties, military, financial and political, finally surmounted and the force demanded by Dean Matthews in actual existence, ready to threaten, to strike and to overwhelm at any point where lawless aggression might raise its head. With our force in existence on a war footing, let us now ask with what feelings would it be regarded by those nations which still counted themselves as free, sovereign and independent? Would it give them the feeling of security or of insecurity? Would it make them feel safe or unsafe in the continued enjoyment of their lives and liberties?

The answer is that it would be a standing menace to the liberty and independence of everyone of them, and its existence—if we can conceive it existing at all—would not be tolerated a moment. Who could answer for the loyalty of the force to the League of Nations? Who could trust it to carry out the mission for which it was created and *to embark on no other?* As defined by Dean Matthews it would be the most powerful fighting force in existence and, as such, in a position to work its will in any direction in which it chose to operate. Who could restrain it? No "madman," you say, would dare to challenge it. Yes: but the overwhelming power which made it unchallengeable by madmen would make it unchallengeable by everybody else. Created to restrain aggression, and furnished with overwhelming power for that purpose, what is to prevent it from becoming aggressive itself and overthrowing the League which created it? It, and not the League, would now be the real ruler of the world. The destinies of all nations would be in its hands.

So we reach this interesting conclusion, that it would be impossible for the League to create the force demanded by the orthodox doctrine without at the same time placing itself and every nation composing it at the mercy of that force. A more unpromising road to collective security could not be imagined.

The further we pursue our enquiry the more lamentable does it seem that so much of the energies of the League, or of its leading supporters, has been expended on the advocacy of this impossible project. No ingenuity, no skill in contrivance can render it practicable. The whole enterprise is off the track on which the pacification of the world, the reconciliation of the nations and the distant unity of mankind can ever be reached; off the track which leads to them, but on the track which leads to confusion and strife. Rarely have wise men been the victims of a stranger aberration.

If an explanation of it can be given, it seems to lie chiefly in the fact that the discussion of world peace has been continually dominated by the false analogy already discussed between the conditions under which the rule of law is maintained within the state and those which obtain in its external relations with other states. A further explanation may perhaps be found in the curious but widely prevalent delusion that collective force, being overwhelming, would win its victories over lawless aggressors by merely *threatening* to fight them, and so stop short of actual violence and bloodshed. Of this delusion it may be said that it could only exist among those who, however wise they may be about collective force, are ignorant of lawless aggressors and their ways.

The strange lengths to which the delusion may run is illustrated by a story overheard by the present writer in the smoking-room of a certain club. At a recent meeting to promote recruiting the chief orator was enlarging on the now familiar and perhaps sound proposition that in the present condition of the world a strongly-armed Britain is the best guarantee of world peace. After making this clear by various arguments the orator proceeded, with admirable logic, to point the moral as follows: "If only you young men would come forward and join the forces, not in twos and threes, but in your thousands and millions, *you would never have to fight*." The result was that only one man joined up. And he was a Quaker.

CHAPTER VII

THE LEAGUE AS FIDUCIARY

AS a well-built city has a plan of its own which is not that of any house within its gates, nor even of the City Hall; or, again, as the human body is not an expanded version of any of its parts, such as a brain, or a hand, an arm or a leg, but reveals in the synthesis of them all a form and a structure which none of them separately has, so it may well be that the true pattern of a League of Nations is not to be found in any one of the nations comprised within its membership. Composed of them it certainly will be. But will it necessarily copy their form, their structure or their function? They are all political states, organised to maintain the rule of law and equipped with means to deal with rebellion by shot and shell. They all possess the fighting sting. Does it follow from this that a League or Union composed of these same nations will be a political institution of the same pattern and equipped in like manner? For reasons already given we think not.

Though the League, as now constituted, is not a super-state, it has nevertheless a tendency in that direction, and may justly be called a political institution. Though unprovided with shot and shell of its own, it yet makes provision, in Article 16, for bringing them to bear on the rebel. It thus possesses the fighting sting which characterises the political state.

The League was created by politicians. They constitute its Council and Assembly; they form the personnel of its committees; they conduct its business; they man its official posts; they act as its spokesmen; they furnish it with oratory. The place of their assembling is Geneva, but the habits of mind they bring with them, their ways of thought, even their ways of speech are those of the Foreign Offices that sent them there and trained them to play their part. All this would not be so unless the League, as it now exists, were a political institution.

We have here no case to make against political institutions, nor against politicians. Immense are the services they have rendered to mankind and will continue to render. The perfect form of government has, indeed, not yet been found; nor has the perfect politician. Man has suffered much at their hands, many wrongs and many woes, but without them he would be, as Plato said, the wildest and most dangerous of all the animals. Let them remain, then; let them keep their fighting stings as long as they have any use for them, which may not be for ever. They have their own destiny to accomplish. But the destiny of the League is different. Its pattern is not theirs.

The final form of the League, and its true form as we here conceive it, is fiduciary. The political states composing it may continue severally to rest upon force, but their *union* will rest upon good faith. In their union they will seek to rest upon nothing else because, as we have seen, there is nothing else to hold them together.

But the fiduciary form will not be suddenly assumed. The League will evolve towards it gradually, but perhaps rapidly, when once the first step has been taken, and good faith frankly acknowledged as the only security. For that acknowledgment, we think, the time is ripe.

As a fiduciary institution the working of the League would be in the hands of trustees. They might be politicians, or they might not; but whether politicians or philosophers, they would represent, not primarily the policy, the wealth or the armed power of the nation from which they came, but its good faith. Their prime qualification would be their trustworthiness. And since that quality is seldom unaccompanied by high gifts of competence and skill, there is ground to hope that their business would be well done. Such men are to be found.

That the League as resting on a fiduciary basis would be free from perils is a claim that can be made for no human institution. "Safety first" is certainly a wiser motto than "danger first," which the apostles of "living dangerously" seem to favour; but it becomes foolish when *absolute* safety is aimed at. There is no such thing in any walk of life, most assuredly not in the path of the peacemaker. No man is absolutely safe until he is dead; no institution until, like the granite mountain in the Arabian desert,* it has passed away into a memory. The choice of the peacemaker's path is a choice between greater perils and less, and will so remain till the end of the chapter. In choosing the path we here indicate the most we can say in its favour is, that here the perils are less than those which beset the alternative, or, more strictly, they are of a different kind—more likely to call forth the best that is in the nations and less likely to call forth the worst. Let us then consider the perils of the alternative and, after that, weigh the two. That done, we shall be nearing our goal.

* It is said that somewhere in that vast solitude there outcrops an enormous massif of granite, or other hard stone, covering many acres, on the face of which some traveller of bygone ages, halting his caravan as he was passing by, has inscribed these words in the Arabic character, at about the height of a man seated on a camel— THIS TOO WILL PASS.

CHAPTER VIII

THE FRAILTY OF ALLIANCES

THAT alliances, treaties and covenants between sovereign states are far more precarious and exposed to infraction than legal contracts between individuals will be generally admitted. Legal contracts are so contrived that any of the parties defaulting in his obligations will get into trouble of one kind or another. Either a security is deposited, subject to forfeit on non-fulfilment, or some other penalty attached. And behind it all stands the law of the land to enforce the penalty if need be.

In the case of treaties, covenants and alliances these safeguards do not exist. Perhaps the most solemn and elaborate treaty ever made was the Covenant of the League of Nations. At one time seventy nations were parties to it. But none of them deposited any security for the fulfilment of its obligations, though many of them had a bad record in the matter of treaty-keeping, while some of the obligations incurred were of a kind which might become, under certain circumstances, a formidable challenge to the good faith of the most loyal.

THE FRAILTY OF ALLIANCES

It is true that the Covenant contained a provision in Article XVI which bound the parties to combine their forces to punish any one of them that turned delinquent. But this only added another obligation to the others, and was just as liable to infraction as those it was intended to protect. Indeed more liable, as the event was soon to prove. In the crisis of last year the Covenant was doubly broken, first by Italy in attacking Abyssinia, and then by some fifty other states in disregarding their obligations to stop her. And there was nothing to prevent the fifty defaulting, nothing corresponding to the law of the land to prosecute the whole lot for breach of contract. Had the situation been covered by the Law of Contracts, with constituted authority to enforce it, Abyssinia would have been in a position to claim enormous damages from those fifty nations. As it was they escaped with impunity. What could better illustrate the futility of such a provision?

Just as these alliances are unprotected by anything corresponding to the Law of Contracts, so they are unprotected by anything corresponding to a gentleman's code of honour. This code requires the gentleman to keep his pledge even when circumstances have so changed that breaking it would pay him better than keeping it. Political states have not yet risen to that. In Ruskin's definition of a gentleman, which it would be hard to improve on, he is one who "swears to his own hurt and changes not," in contrast to the devil who, when he is sick, resolves to turn monk and breaks his resolution as soon as his health improves.* Needless to say, international ethics, in the matter of treaty-keeping, are nearer to the devil's code than to the gentleman's. With recent events fresh in mind we can hardly regard these treaties as deserving the name of gentlemen's agreements. If some of the parties have the gentleman's habit of keeping his word, all of them certainly have not. Some of them, if judged by their record in keeping their pledges, even those given in recent years, would fall into a category poles asunder from Ruskin's definition. In drawing up their covenants political states give themselves a name which suggests that they are under some illusion in this matter. They call themselves the "High Contracting Parties." It is a misleading term. If a history of broken treaties were to be written it would be found that all of these High Contracting Parties are miserable sinners, though in various degrees. It would be no unfitting thing if the next European Conference were to begin with a "general confession" to that effect.

The frailty of alliances is further increased by the mutability of the governments that are parties to them. It is only under their geographical

---

* "The devil was sick; the devil a monk would be;
 The devil was well; the devil a monk was he."—RABELAIS.

names, Britain, France, Germany, Russia and the rest that the contracting governments retain a fairly continuous identity. In the geographical sense the nations called upon to fulfil the Covenant in 1935 were almost identical with the nations which signed it in 1919. But the governments were all different, with new personnel, new policies, new tempers and new aims. Some of them, notably the French, had been changed many times and in other countries, such as Germany and Italy, there had been political revolutions. Revolutionary governments are not in the habit of honouring commitments made by the governments they have overthrown, not even to the extent of paying their debts.* For this reason all alliances made with states liable to revolution, and not many are wholly safe from it, are fundamentally insecure. And even when the changes of government take place constitutionally as from one political party to another, the strength of existing alliances cannot fail to be affected. In spite of the maxim that treaties entered into by a party government are binding on its successors in power, it is obvious that a treaty will be kept in a very different spirit according as the successors are or are not in sympathy with the foreign policy under which it was originally made.

If now we assemble the points mentioned—the

---

* This kind of default is not confined to revolutionary governments.

lack of security against non-fulfilment, the equal lack of a code of honour sufficiently binding to insure fulfilment, the bad record of many nations in the matter of treaty-keeping, the unblemished record of none of them, the mutability of all the contracting governments and the instability of some—putting all that together we have a set of conditions which no lawyer would tolerate in drawing up a contract between individuals, even between accredited gentlemen. Few things on this planet would cause more astonishment to an impartial observer of human affairs than the persistence of the belief that security can be established by negotiating treaties under these conditions. Their history follows a fairly uniform line. They last only so long as fulfilment is not difficult but begin to totter the moment default appears more advantageous than fulfilment to one or other of the parties. In other words, they are wont to last only so long as they are not needed. A "history of broken treaties," if it ever comes to be written, will confirm this, even if confined to the period between the Holy Alliance and Locarno. The Covenant of the League would probably be the outstanding instance.

So far we have been dealing with alliances in general. We pass on to those in which the military character is predominant. A military alliance is one which binds the parties to make common war, usually defensive war, under specified circumstances.

If such a contract is to be fulfilled it is obvious that the parties to it must keep themselves in readiness for fulfilment and in equal readiness. That is so if only two nations, say Britain and France, are involved. If these two make a compact to combine in resisting an attack, and one of them keeps its powder dry while the other does not, the attack may fall at a moment when the less ready nation is less inclined than the other to keep its word. There is no telling how public opinion in the less ready nation will compel its government to act. Will regard for the sanctity of the treaty triumph over the unwillingness of the nation to enter on a war for which it has neglected to make adequate preparation? We all remember the uncertainties of 1914, and the agonised interviews between Sir Edward Grey and M. Cambon at the Foreign Office. We were under treaty obligations to defend the integrity of Belgium, but our preparations for resisting its violation by Germany were less advanced than those of our ally, though hers, perhaps, were not adequate. For days it was touch and go. The Great War was a war of precarious alliances fought over the ruins of a broken treaty,* and the tragic "peace" which followed gave birth to a series

* Broken by Germany.

of treaties all of which have since been broken.

This element of frailty, which is apparent enough when only two nations are involved, increases progressively as more nations are brought into the alliance. It may be said to have reached its maximum last year when some fifty nations found themselves confronted with an obligation which required them to make common war, first economic and then military, upon an aggressor. How many of the nations which had bound themselves under Article XVI to take warlike action against the aggressor had kept themselves in readiness, to say nothing of equal readiness, to fulfil that obligation against an aggressor so powerful and so unexpected as Italy? How many of them were willing to do so? They were all in a situation which threatened to drag them into war against their will, and yet confronted with an obligation to that effect. With the terrible alternative before them between breaking their pledge and becoming involved in war for which they were unprepared, and which none of them wanted, they preferred the former. They defaulted in their obligation to stop Mussolini.

What else was to be expected? Nations which bind themselves to make common war against aggression or anything else, and yet neglect to keep themselves constantly ready and willing to fulfil that obligation under any circumstances where fulfilment may be called for, are simply breaking their pledges in advance. In 1936 the nations of the League were like the crew of a lifeboat suddenly called to the rescue of a sinking ship, with their lifeboat not yet built, the crew widely scattered, the men untrained to row together, most of them out of condition and all of them unwilling to risk their lives on the stormy waters just then and there. They had undertaken more than they were capable of performing. To rebuke them for their common default and give them lectures on the sanctity of treaties is surely beside the mark. And which of them is to be the lecturer? Which of them is entitled to play the part of Pharisee to the others' Publican? In 1936 did they not *all* leave the sinking ship to her fate?

Yet another cause of frailty, which has grown very active in recent days, arises from the nature of modern weapons. Covenant or no covenant all governments are growing more and more reluctant to expose their civil populations to methods of warfare which could only be decently employed for the extermination of noxious vermin. These methods, moreover, have largely obliterated the difference between victory and defeat. If employed in any major war the result is likely to be destruction for both sides. In spite of the warlike talk indulged in by certain governments, there can be little doubt that the fear of war, greatly intensified by these causes, is everywhere stronger than the desire for war, and is probably the best safeguard of peace at the present moment. What is the effect of this on military alliances? When the circumstances arise which require a number of nations to run the risks of modern war under the terms of their alliance, may we not count with certainty on one or more doing their best to evade the obligation?

We may note further that even when nations go to war under the terms of an alliance their governments seldom make good companions in arms. Their fighting men may do so, but not their governments. Disputes as to strategy, jealousies in the High Command, accusations that one or other is not pulling its weight, fears that this one or that will make a separate peace, as Russia did—had we not enough of all that during the Great War?

Finally the question may be raised whether the term "sanctity" can be properly applied to any treaty which binds a nation to become involved in the wholesale massacre into which modern war has degenerated. Any pledge to that effect is an oath given to the devil and is sacred only in the sense that the devil demands its fulfilment.

Much more might be said to the same effect, but let this suffice. The conclusion to be drawn from it may be expressed in a parody of familiar words—"Frailty, thy name is a military alliance." Nothing durable in that direction, least of all a durable peace!

CHAPTER IX

VAIN EXPECTATIONS

IF a strong and well-armed man were to allow an abominable outrage on a defenceless person to be committed under his eyes by a ruffian, and make no attempt to save the victim, even at the cost of risking his life in combat with the ruffian, should we not condemn him as a coward and feel ourselves disgraced if he were a member of our family? Such a thing the world saw not long ago. A group of nations, strongly armed enough, our own among them, when confronted by an abominable outrage on a well-nigh defenceless state, allowed it to proceed, with the aggravation added that all of them were under a pledge to come to the rescue of the victim, by mortal combat if need be. Are we justified in condemning these nations or their governments, as many have done, for cowardice and perfidy, and in feeling ourselves humiliated if one of the nations so condemned happens to be our own?

To escape from the feeling of humiliation is impossible and to argue against it would be futile. But possibly we are wrong in making scapegoats of the governments who allowed this thing to happen.

CO-OPERATION OR COERCION?

Here we are in the presence of a very difficult problem. Are the standards by which we judge our own conduct and that of other men applicable to sovereign states in their dealings one with another? Can it be justly said that in whatever circumstances an individual may be condemned as a coward or a traitor, a state or a government must be condemned in the same terms? This problem, which has exercised the wits of many, we here make no attempt to solve. But we shall call attention to certain facts which are relevant both to it and to our own subject.

We note in the first place that accusations brought against governments for weakness, irresolution, perfidy, double-dealing, tergiversation and similar vices of foreign policy, clearly imply that the state, in its dealing with other states, may be justly expected to conform its conduct to the standards which the accusers apply to themselves and to other men. The question whether states are capable of so acting causes no hesitation and is, in fact, not raised. It is taken for granted that they are capable.

In the next place we may observe that whatever capacity the political state may have for the virtues opposite to the vices just named, there is one virtue, highly esteemed among individuals and adorned with many illustrious examples, for which, so far, it has shown no capacity whatsoever. This is the virtue of self-renunciation, the virtue of making itself a sacrifice to the good of other states, of giving its life, so to say, as a ransom for many. There is no record in history of any sovereign state willing to make such a sacrifice of itself, though the greatest of the Jewish Prophets did apparently contemplate it as the high destiny of his own nation.* The birth in any state of a capacity for conduct of this kind in its foreign policy would be a new phenomenon in the history of international morals. Many states have played the part of Judas: none that of Christ.

Let us vary our question. We praise the man who risks his life to save a companion from drowning, even though his life be far more valuable to society than the life of the man he tries to save. But would praise be given by the British people to those responsible for the safety of the Empire if they were to risk it for the purely benevolent purpose of saving from destruction another state less valuable than itself, or at least deemed less valuable by the British? And would the statesmen who take such decisions be justly chargeable with betraying their trust if they declined the risk? Were the statesmen in question called upon to risk their personal safety and nothing more, the answer would be simple enough. But how stands the matter when we remember that the whole British Empire, with its four hundred million inhabitants, is involved in the risk taken? Even

---

* Isaiah liii.

so, the idealist might answer, our statesmen would be worthy of praise if they took the risk, and of blame if they refused it. But would the British public, admirer of heroism though it be, agree with the idealist in deeming such action heroic? Or would they condemn it as a betrayal of trust and promptly find other statesmen to rule over them?

From all this we conclude that in the present state of international morals any form of Covenant which commits the participating states to a self-renouncing line of action is likely to prove beyond their capacity and to be broken when the hour for fulfilment arrives. Expectations to the contrary are vain.

The Covenant of the League commits the participating states to wage collective warfare on the unjust aggressor, and to do so in the name of the international justice which is the common cause of them all. What does this involve? It clearly assumes in each of the participating states a self-renouncing disposition, or capacity for self-sacrifice, comparable to that of the hero bringing in a wounded man on the battlefield, or the lifeboat crew going out to a sinking ship in a hurricane. No state can go to war collectively or otherwise for any cause whatsoever without willingness to shed the blood of its nationals, expend their treasure, and imperil the vital interests of the body politic. It has to be remembered also that any state going to war against another thereby exposes its flank to other aggressors, of whom more than one may be waiting for precisely that opportunity, with all the risks of a spreading conflagration. To suppose that political states would be willing to incur these formidable perils on behalf of some victim or cause not directly involving their own interest is to conceive them as having adopted the code of chivalry in their mutual relations. It assumes, at least, that international altruism has reached the level attained by the Good Samaritan, if not that of the Round Table.*

This, as recent events clearly prove, is an overestimate of the self-renouncing disposition of sovereign political states. Had Abyssinia, like Antwerp, been "a pistol pointed at the head of England" or at the head of any other Great Power, there would have been a very different story to tell. As it was, no Good Samaritan came to her rescue when fallen among thieves, no Knight of the Round Table risked his life to save her from outrage, no Grace Darling put out to the sinking ship—though many were

---

* It is interesting to compare the two standards, especially in connection with our present subject. Had a Knight of the Round Table encountered the man fallen among thieves, he would probably have done all that the Good Samaritan did and something more. After depositing his man at the inn he would have remounted his horse, returned to the scene of the outrage, tracked the robbers to their lair and taught them a lesson.

pledged so to do. It was the misfortune of Abyssinia to point no pistol at any powerful head.

If further evidence to the same effect be demanded, the recent doings of sovereign states on the field of economic policy will furnish it in abundance. From the day the Covenant was signed until now the covenanting states, with hardly an exception, have been busily engaged in building tariff walls, each for the protection of its own interest, with no regard whatever to the damage thereby inflicted on the interests of its neighbours. Not much of the Good Samaritan in that department and still less of the Round Table! To expect that nations governed by self-regard so reckless of foreign interest in their economic relations will be ready, at the call of justice and fair play, to shed their blood and spend their treasure altruistically when any one of them happens to become the object of unjust aggression can only be described as an astonishing overestimate of their present capacity for that species of virtue. Yet is it not precisely on such an overestimate that Article XVI of the Covenant was founded? Does not that Article clearly commit the covenanting nations, or their governments, to self-renouncing action far beyond their present powers of fulfilment? Would any existing government, cabinet, or body of statesmen, holding the position of trustees for the life and fortunes of a nation, take the responsibility of exposing them to the manifold risks of warfare in a cause which was none of its own? Would the ruling government of any of them be held justified by its own nationals in so doing? What would be the fate of any statesman or political party rash enough to propose it? Individuals can act in this manner, and often do so; corporate states, never. Can we wonder, then, that a Covenant binding them to such action turns out in the day of performance to be little better than a paralysing entanglement which, far from restraining the aggressor, seems rather to give him the opportunity he is waiting for?

How does our own country stand in this matter? Without raising the question whether we are more or less benevolently disposed to our neighbours than they to us—a question on which the views of foreigners might differ considerably from our own—let us ask, in the first place, what the position of the British Empire would be were it to become the object of aggression by some foreign power, Germany, Japan, or any other? How many of the fifty-odd nations adhering to the Covenant could be relied on to fulfil their covenanted obligation to combine forces for our defence, and to incur the risk to themselves involved in so doing? Exactly how many no man can tell. But may we not say with complete confidence that our only friends in the day of peril would be those who found it to their own interest to befriend us—those, namely, who deem their own safety involved in the preservation of ours? If Abyssinia, ill able to defend herself, has been deserted in the day of her peril by so many who were pledged to defend her, is it likely that they would all rally as one man to the defence of the mighty British Empire? We know very well that nothing of the kind would happen. Our statesmen know it. Why else do they tell us that our Air Force must be equal to that of any other single power? Why else must our contribution to collective security be on such a scale of armament as to render us independent of collective security in the event of the others deserting us—as all deserted Abyssinia?

Reversing the picture, let us now imagine the British Empire called upon, under the terms of a Covenant, to resist aggression on one of our European fellow-covenanters—an attack by Germany upon Austria or by Japan on the Soviet Republic or any other of the numerous "attacks" now deemed possible or likely. Is there any reason to suppose that our policy would not repeat what we did (or refrained from doing) in the test case of Abyssinia—unless, indeed, it were evident that the attack we were called on to resist was an indirect attack on ourselves? Would the British Government embark on the conflict, or the British public approve of their so embarking, merely as a redressor of wrong done to Austria or Russia, or as a champion of international justice in general? Or if it were alleged that such action could only be taken "within the framework of the collective system," would not the said framework be found in the day of performance to be the same paralysing entanglement we found it in the recent crisis, and should not we have again to confess, to our shame and dismay, that action within the "framework" was little better than inaction called by another name? Perhaps the answer to these questions may best be given in words written by Mr. Gladstone in 1869:

> "Is England so uplifted in strength that she can with prudence advertise herself as ready to undertake the general redress of wrongs? Would not the consequence of such professions and promises be either the premature exhaustion of her means or a collapse in the day of performance?"*

What more is needed to explain the collapse of the League "in the day of performance" when Abyssinia, fallen among thieves, called for the fulfilment of Article XVI?

How comes it to pass, we may well ask, that this inevitable result was unforeseen? The explanation lies in a pair of connected illusions which still

---

* Morley's *Life of Gladstone*, volume 3, page 317, quoted by Mr. Alwyn Parker in *The Times*, May 23rd, 1936.

hold their ground in face of events which have proved them false. The first is the odd assumption that no more than one aggressor would have to be dealt with at a time. The other is the belief, already referred to, that the combination of armed force represented by the covenanting states would be so overwhelming that no single aggressor would dare to challenge it; that the mere *threat* of it would be enough and, therefore, that the peacekeepers would never be driven to the extremity of implementing their pledge by shedding their own or the aggressor's blood. This satisfies the pacifist supporter of the League. When faced by the objection that he is false to his principles in supporting a scheme which might eventuate in bloodshed he can always reply, "Not so: the scheme I support is so contrived that it will be automatically arrested at the stage of a threat; there will be no shedding of blood but only a brandishing of irresistible arms in the aggressor's face."

A queer reply, to be sure, but the substance of which we have often heard repeated. And, naturally, having started with the assumption that collective force, by reason of its overwhelming preponderance, will remain perpetually at the stage of a threat, no consideration is given to what might happen to it in the extreme case of having to face the aggressor on the battlefield—the possibility, namely, that it might not prove so overwhelming after all, that its composite character would render it exceptionally vulnerable both to hostile strategy and to political intrigue, and that a powerful aggressor, with a couple of million men behind him and a military genius to lead them, might conceivably make short work of it. Powerful aggressors are not so easily terrorised, especially when more than one of them happen to be active at the same time.

CHAPTER X

THE WAR-MACHINE

IF the professions of European statesmen are to be accepted at their face value, it would appear that in each and all of them there exists a strong desire to establish the peace of Europe on a firm basis. Why, then, the plain man is constantly asking, do they appear so impotent in the matter? The answer is that the war machinery, in the working of which these statesmen have become involved, is more powerful than their peaceable intentions. It has an energy, a momentum, an organisation, a technical efficiency which the peacemaking forces have not. There is a common saying that in these days machines rule the world. The machine which rules foreign policy is the war-machine, never so powerful as now. Ostensibly the machinery is controlled by the governments; in reality the governments, though they do not always know it, are controlled by the machinery. Like the dagger in *Macbeth*, it marshals them the way that they are going. Thus the answer to the plain man's question reduces itself to a single word—"armaments," understood in the wide sense of the war-machine and the fighting forces that work it.

Whether it be true or false that the armament of our own country, considered by itself, is a force that makes for peace—as we are constantly assured—there can be no doubt that armaments taken in their ever-mounting *totality*, to which this country is now making so massive a contribution, are a force that makes for war. Great Britain is not alone among the Great Powers in representing her armament as an instrument for the preservation of peace, in accordance with the maxim *si vis pacem, para bellum*. But this maxim, true though it may be of a particular nation at a particular moment, is patently false when applied to a group of quarrelsome nations, all preparing for *bellum* at the same time. Under those conditions the *bellum* they are preparing for is bound in the long run to be the end of the matter.

An armament, no matter for which purpose it may have been created, is equally available for attack or defence, and though honestly designed for the latter purpose only, there is no assurance that it will not be used, in some moment of passion or of national crisis, for the former. Owing to this, the peaceable professions of statesmen are apt to be interpreted as masking some sinister design. We have only to recall the attitude of an important section of the British Press to the peace-keeping professions of Herr Hitler to realise how little confidence such professions inspire in a world of continuously mounting armaments. And there is abundant evidence that the similar professions of our own statesmen are seldom interpreted abroad in the sense intended by their authors. In the eye of the foreigner (to judge by the comments in the foreign Press) Great Britain is arming, not for the purpose of keeping the peace but, somewhat less benevolently, for the purpose of keeping what she has got. If somebody would invent a type of armament which could be used only for defence but not for attack, for keeping the peace but not for breaking it, and if all the Powers great and small were to arm themselves exclusively with that type of weapon, the growth of armaments might go on to any extent without endangering the peace of the world or giving rise to the least suspicion. But so long as armaments retain their double character—and there is no prospect that they will ever lose it—their continual growth will have a sterilising effect on all peacekeeping professions, no matter by whom uttered.

To understand the significance of armaments they must be viewed in their totality. They will then be seen to constitute an enormous warmachine dominating the life of nations, and driving it in the direction of war; the parts so interrelated that when one starts into action the whole begins to move. Nothing could be more absurd than to suppose that the totality of the world's armaments can be so manipulated, by treaties or diplomatic arts, as to suppress its own activities as a war-making instrument and convert it into an instrument for keeping the peace.

This was the error into which the authors of the Covenant unwittingly fell. They invoked Satan to cast Satan out. Their plan, reduced to its lowest terms, was to put an end to aggressive war-making by an overpowering combination of war-making forces. The result was that the League of Nations itself became deeply involved in the war-machine, whose operations it aimed to suppress; fell under its domination, and found, at the first crisis that called for the application of the plan, that it was on the very brink of war.

The way, moreover, was opened for a pernicious form of make-believe. Each nation in the League, the principals at all events, while arming for such independent belligerency as its own interests may demand (the real motive in every case), could now pretend that its armaments were intended as a benevolent contribution to collective security, and under cover of that pretext proceed to arm itself to the teeth in competition with the others doing the same thing under the same cover—an element of dishonesty which deceives nobody and merely serves to taint the atmosphere with new elements of fear and mistrust.

Armaments are inseparably connected with the

principle of national sovereignty. Each armament represents the determination of the state which owns it to be master in its own house and arbiter of its own destiny, a determination progressively more assertive as the state increases in power and wealth. For this reason, armaments are, of all the possessions of a sovereign state, the least susceptible of being pooled for any common purpose.

All sovereign states are, in the last analysis, war-making institutions. Though not always fighting nor always even bellicose, their combative functions are so closely integrated with their general structure that they cannot be isolated for repressive treatment. Like the wasp, the sovereign state has a fighting sting, which is no external attachment to be shed at will, but organically united to the body politic as a whole. The advance of science, far from removing this characteristic, has greatly intensified it; and Christianity has had no success in arresting the process.

It is noteworthy that on the very day—March 16th, 1937—when three or four orators in the House of Commons went out of their way to declare that British armaments are intended only for the preservation of peace, General Göring in Berlin was justifying German armaments on precisely the same ground. From which it should be evident that the rhetorical dedication of armaments to peace has no effect whatever in checking the race for them, useful though it be for placating the Nonconformist conscience and making it easier for our patriotic Bishops to reconcile the function of armaments (provided they are British) with the teaching of Christianity.

But would not the case be more fairly stated, and our bona fides less suspected abroad, if we abandoned our attempts to invest British rearmament with the air of a philanthropic enterprise and claimed no other motive for it than the very proper one of protecting our highly vulnerable Empire from attack? Other nations could hardly criticise us for doing so, since all of them are no less determined than the British to keep what they have got. It may be true, as foreigners are fond of reminding us, that much of our Empire has been acquired by conquest of a more or less aggressive character, but that is no reason why we should allow the said foreigners to conquer it for themselves. There seems to be an opportunity for the British Government to give a lead in practising this kind of candour: it would certainly clear the air and put an end to a great deal of highly pernicious cant. No doubt our armed strength wins us a certain kind of respect; but we should be respected still more, and in a higher sense, if we overcame our inveterate habit of inventing moral reasons for looking after our own interests.

Before proceeding to the second part of our task it may be well to summarise the conclusions which emerge from the line of thought we have been pursuing.

(1) That in the present state of international morality there is no infallible method of preventing war. The utmost we can hope for, or profitably aim at, is to render war progressively less attractive to war-makers.

(2) That all treaties, compacts, or covenants to suppress war by a general combination of armed force endure only so long as their application is not needed and are certain to collapse in the day of performance.

(3) That no future Covenant adopting the above method is likely to yield better results than its ill-starred predecessor, or to be anything else than the old medicine in a new bottle.

(4) That, therefore, the League of Nations, if it is to continue, must cease to be predominantly a League of *armed* nations and find for itself a new direction no longer dominated by war-making considerations, leaving these latter to be dealt with by whatever agencies exist for the purpose.

(5) That the new line of direction should aim at the creation of a common interest, at once co-operative in basis and business-like in pursuit.

(6) That in pursuing this new line of action efforts should be concentrated, at first, on establishing a nucleus for positive co-operation, a

THE WAR-MACHINE

nucleus likely to grow and by its growth to act as an increasing deterrent on war.

(7) That such an enterprise, if wisely conceived, would, even in its inception, be one of considerable magnitude, and such as to challenge both then and afterwards the best talent of the covenanting nations.

(8) That in framing the requisite Covenant to embody these aims no higher demand should be made on the altruism of sovereign political states than is customary in business transactions or contracts intended for the mutual benefit of the contracting parties.

PART II - CONSTRUCTIVE

CHAPTER XI

THE MOST PROMISING INSTITUTION IN THE WORLD

WERE there in existence a universal Church in which men of all races and ways of thinking could find their spiritual home and unite in one fellowship of loyalty and good-will, it would be unquestionably the world's most valuable institution. That Church does not at present exist, though the possibility is not to be ruled out that one day it may come into being. Pending its arrival—if it is to arrive—the world's most valuable institution to-day is the League of Nations. It is so, not in virtue of what it has already accomplished, though this if fairly judged is not inconsiderable, but in virtue of the promise it holds, of that to which it points forward. To say that the fortunes of humanity on this planet are closely bound up with its preservation and development is no exaggeration. It may even be that out of it there will arise in the course of ages that universal fellowship of loyalty and good-will, that Church of Humanity, in which all men will find their spiritual home. At present the League is little more than an acorn newly planted; but its destiny, if wisely tended, is to grow into a mighty tree. Unwisely tended it may die, or it may perish through apathy and neglect. That would be an immeasurable calamity. This book is written in the hope that it may be averted.

The foundation of the League was a novel experiment in human history. Its designs were on a vaster scale than statesmanship had ever before coped with, and the experience needed to achieve them was, in consequence, lacking. The ground was new, the region unmapped. Unknown forces had been summoned into operation and problems, successfully solved in the narrower fields of national life, were now transferred to the international field, where they became so changed that the former solutions no longer applied. The way had to be found by the method of trial and error. The League was like a child learning to walk. Mistakes were inevitable, and only a false shame will prevent us confessing them.

The chief mistake was the attempt to impose upon sovereign states a system of coercion which their nature as sovereign forbids them to tolerate. It was a natural mistake in those who had yet to learn—for the attempt had never been made before—that sovereign states cannot be brought under discipline by methods applicable to peaceable citizens long trained in the habit of submission to the law. Perfectly intelligible after the event, the error could hardly have been foreseen until the event had revealed it. That revelation has now taken place and is, we think, decisive.

It seems to have been forgotten that the law-abiding habit of an ordered society is the result of a long historical process. It is not by the simple act of signing a covenant to keep the peace and to combine in restraining the peacebreaker that you and I have learnt to pay heed to constituted authority and to refrain from shooting the tax-collector when he brings his unwelcome demands to our doors. Our habits of submission are a social inheritance from centuries of discipline in which our fathers were gradually broken in to accept the yoke, until paying tribute to Cæsar became, as it were, a second nature. The sovereign states of the world have no such inheritance; they are untamed to the yoke; the discipline that would have tamed them has never been theirs. Since the fall of the Holy Roman Empire there has been no common authority even in Europe. Until the League of Nations appeared the attempt to bring them under the yoke had never been made. Like the lawless barons of old, the only régime they have acknowledged, if régime it may be called, is one which leaves them unquestioned masters in their own houses, well-ordered or ill-ordered as these may be. They are unaccustomed to any rule of law save that of their own governments; their armies have never taken orders to march, nor their navies to sail, from other headquarters. If one of them would enforce its will on another, as by saying to it, "Withdraw your armies from my frontiers and dismantle your fortifications," the demand is treated as an ultimatum and answered with a declaration of war. And if the matter be further enquired into, it will be found that the process by which heptarchies have been united into single kingdoms and fighting factions taught to keep the peace has never had in view a general federation of the nations or pointed forward to any such consummation. As pointed out in a former chapter, it has been prompted throughout by the need of domestic solidarity in pursuing a policy of conquest or in resisting the designs of the foreign conqueror, either or both.

Such are the habits and traditions of sovereign states. Such are the conditions under which, as we might say, they have been brought up. Each pays tribute to its own Cæsar, and to no other; each obeys the rule of law laid down for it in its own constitution, and in no other. To bow down before a greater Cæsar, or accept a wider rule of law would involve a change of nature in every one of them. Those who imagine that this can be brought about by the mere act of signing a covenant to that effect imagine the impossible. The leopard cannot change his spots so easily nor the Ethiopian his skin.

None the less the truth is indisputable that until a wider rule of law is accepted by the nations there will be no durable peace on the earth. But the approach must be from a different angle, on a different ground, in a different atmosphere and by a different method. *Forced* into accepting that wider rule the nations cannot be, not even by a collective preponderance of strength, all attempts in that direction merely serving to stiffen their resistance. But *educated* into accepting it they may be; and this, as we shall endeavour to show, is the great task awaiting the League.

Strange as it may seem in presence of the majestic doings and pretensions of these "High Contracting Powers," their international morality —another name for their acceptance of the rule of law in their mutual relations—is still barbaric. At that point their education has hardly begun. Whatever else may be civilised, that remains uncivilised. But there must be no forcing of the issue, no attempt to achieve at a bound that which can only be achieved when the willingness exists to practise patience and endure reverses without losing heart. In the words of a thinker whom we shall quote more fully later on, "the best teaching of international morality must remain, for the present, *indirect*." Not by defining the law, nor by creating machinery for enforcing it, nor by exhortation to its observance will the League fulfil the function we would assign it: that of a grand Training School for the nations in the art and practice of international co-operation. The

League will devise the forms of this, supervise their activities and administer the resources needed to promote them, preaching less and practising more. In this way its teaching of international morality will be, for the present, indirect, and practical rather than theoretical. Operating on these lines it will justify the claim we have made for it as the most promising institution now extant on the earth.

The League has recently received a shattering blow—the penalty of its first mistake. But all will be well if the mistake is confessed, the effort to perpetuate it abandoned and the lesson it teaches taken to heart. Taught by this experience the League's apparent downfall will mark the hour of rebirth, of resuscitation, of entry on a great work of human beneficence.

The history of the League during the eighteen years of its existence has been no history of failure. It has done most valuable work in many directions. It has promoted international social service of many kinds. It may even claim to have prevented several wars; the Græco-Bulgarian frontier crisis, the boundary dispute between Peru and Colombia, the Saar controversy, the quarrel between Yugoslavia and Hungary arising out of the assassination of King Alexander are the cases in question. *But it will be noted that in none of these beneficent activities, not even in those which are claimed to have prevented war, was the fatal mistake committed of threatening the states concerned with armed coercion.*

In the Abyssinian crisis, the threat signally failed to effect its purpose, though there are those who still believe that, if resolutely carried out, Mussolini would have yielded to it. Such predictions as to what would have happened if sanctions had been pressed home, like all predictions of the "would have" variety, are rash enough. Somewhat less rash, perhaps, is the counter-prediction that far better results would have followed if no threat had been made and sanctions not mentioned at all. Those who incline to this view seem at least entitled to say that if no attempt had been made to coerce Italy the actual result could hardly have been worse than it is; the humiliation of the League would not have been greater, the injustice to Abyssinia not more outrageous, and the general infusion of bad blood into international relationships not more deplorable. On all these fronts the counter-prediction would seem to have some little advantage over the others, rash as all such predictions necessarily are. Be that as it may, the fact should be carefully noted, as a valuable guide to the future development of the League, that its past successes, which have been many and valuable, have followed a line where sanctions were *not* invoked.

CHAPTER XII

FIGHTING NOT ONE OF ITS FUNCTIONS

CONCEIVED and born of political parentage it was to be expected, as we have seen, that the form and structure of the League would reproduce the features of the sovereign state, of which politicians are the servants and to whose methods they are accustomed. With such antecedents and origin something resembling a system of government with fighting forces at its disposal, if not actually in its possession, was bound to make its appearance. To minds trained in the political school it would hardly occur that in constructing a *League* of Nations a wide departure would have to be made from the principles and methods on which the political life of any single nation was conducted. Nor would the need of such a departure occur to the public. The ordinary citizen, accustomed to obey the law and to see its penalties enforced on the disobedient, would naturally tend to think that troublesome sovereign states must be kept in order by the same methods. Neither by him nor by his political leaders would this be recognised as mistaken until actual experiment had proved it so.

Two experiments bearing on the matter are now on record, in the first of which Japan was the delinquent state and in the second Italy. From these experiments two results, clearly connected, have emerged; the one, which was to be expected, that sovereign states are intolerant of coercion; the other, not so foreseeable, that states on which the duty of coercion falls are extremely reluctant to fulfil it. Between this intolerance of coercion on the part of the delinquent and this reluctance to coerce on the part of the others the coercing project inevitably came to grief.

There are those who attribute this collapse to the want of courage and resolution in the coercing party and hold them entirely responsible for the result. To our thinking, the explanation lies deeper. As we see the matter, the coercing party found that they had unwittingly committed themselves to a line of action which their nature as sovereign states forbids them to take, no less than the delinquent states are forbidden by the same nature to submit to such action even if the others were to take it. The truth stood revealed that the wrong model had been chosen. This is not surprising in an enterprise where the way had to be found by the method of trial and error.

In a previous chapter we have considered the false analogy which has misled the discussion of these matters from the outset by inducing the belief that the law-enforcing relation of the state to its own citizens can be reproduced in the relation between a League of sovereign states and the particular states composing it. Instead of reproducing that structure the mission of the League, we here submit, is to create for the nations a new model of community life in which fighting force plays no part whatsoever. Let the fighting function remain with those to whom it belongs, the sovereign political states, until, under the growth of common interests among the nations, it gradually dies a natural death. For them it may be necessary, at least for the time being. To a League aiming at peace it would be fatal. We deprecate the suppression of war by any kind of fighting procedure, believing that all such attempts merely serve to endow war with new vitality and confirm the dominance of the war-machine.

On what, then, the reader will naturally ask, will your New Model depend for the fulfilment of the obligations into which the members of it have entered? How, with no "sword" to restrain the forces which would wreck it, can it proceed to the achievement of any purpose whatsoever?

The answer to this question can be given without hesitation, and will cause surprise only to those whose reflection on these matters has been arrested at some half-way point. Our League will depend simply and solely on the good faith of its members; and this for the reason already given, that, frame the League how you will, it has, and can have, nothing else to depend upon.

Would it not be well, therefore, to realise this from the outset and proclaim it openly? And seeing that good faith is our only security, would it not be well also to pitch the operations of the League in a field where habits and traditions of good faith are relatively well established and avoid the field—that of military compacts—where political states are notoriously given to changing their minds, suspecting each other's loyalties, breaking their bonds and deserting their allies the moment they discover that they have made a bad bargain, or are likely to get the worst of it.

In the present imbroglio of world affairs the announcement by the League that it was resolved to pursue its mission unarmed, and rely on nothing else than the good faith of its members— as, in truth, there is nothing else to rely on—would be a stroke like the cutting of the Gordian knot. Let it use "the sword" for that purpose and for no other. As a mere gesture it would be a service of incalculable value to the cause of peace. The poisonous atmosphere of censoriousness and suspicion would begin to disperse. A wholesome wind would arise. Nor would that be all. Many things of great importance, now impossible, would then become possible. Among them, and perhaps the chief, the way would then be open for the United States, whose partnership in the

FIGHTING NOT ONE OF ITS FUNCTIONS

League is essential to its success, but definitely barred so long as the fighting function is retained, to reconsider their present attitude of abstention and to throw their mighty weight into the cause of world reconciliation.

Those of us who hold these views are often reproached with "leaving the cause of peace with nothing better to fall back upon than the old system of military alliances." We, for our part, are not unwilling to bear the reproach, in the sense that we regard the old system, unsatisfactory though it be, as vastly preferable to the alternative proposed by the coercionists, that, namely, of a military alliance on the grand scale of all the nations now included in the League. Military alliances of the old and limited type are, indeed, frail instruments and dangerous into the bargain. But they have some value as interim means for keeping the peace, and may be allowed to continue as something more than amusement for diplomacy until, as international co-operation develops on other than fighting lines, the need for them dies a natural death. Meanwhile we are unable to see that a military alliance comprising a multitude of nations—say, fifty or more—is an improvement, from any point of view, on an alliance comprising only two or three. On the contrary, we regard it as representing the military alliance at its maximum frailty, with all the dangers inherent in that type of compact accentuated and multiplied in proportion to the number of states involved.

It would seem, therefore, that the orthodox conception of the League as a military alliance on the great or the universal scale stands, in one important respect, on the same level with the non-fighting institution we would have it become. Both depend in the last resort on nothing else than the good faith of the parties. But the former has the disadvantage by operating in a field where good faith is notoriously deficient. And even were it true that a non-fighting League would leave the cause of peace with no alternative but to fall back on the old system of military alliances, which is not altogether valueless, it were surely better to do this than to fall forward into a military alliance conceived on a scale which ensures its collapse in a crisis.

CHAPTER XIII

TYPE OF A GOOD INTERNATIONAL BARGAIN

"We are to bethink us that the Epic is not *Arms and the Man* but *Tools and the Man*—an infinitely wider kind of Epic."—CARLYLE.

"BEGIN to make visible the community of mankind, not merely, as at present, in the form of alliances which are ambiguous, and at times irritating, and of arbitration treaties which are likely to be broken at some passionate moment when they are most needed, but in the form of a sufficiently large board of financially expert trustees, whose membership is international, whose services are duly compensated from the funds of the trust, and whose conduct is guided by plainly stated rules which have the substantially unanimous consent of all nations concerned in the plan."

The above are the words of a distinguished philosopher. They are to be found in a book bearing the title *War and Insurance*,* written soon after the outbreak of the Great War by Josiah Royce, Professor of Philosophy in Harvard

---

* The Macmillan Company, 1914. An article on Royce's philosophy by Paul E. Johnson appeared in the *Hibbert Journal* for July, 1935.

University, a Gifford Lecturer, and the author of many well-known philosophical works.

The sentence quoted reveals our philosopher as doubting the peacekeeping value of political compacts between armed nations. None the less he was in full sympathy with the general project of the League of Nations which was in the air at the time his book was written. It fell into line with a thesis, at once religious and philosophical, to the establishment of which he devoted philosophical powers of no mean order. He was wont to describe his thesis as "the Hope of the Great Community," and to argue that in this hope, and in the action to which it leads, we find both the anchor of religious belief and the fulfilment of our vocation as human beings. The whole duty of man, as he conceived it, is summed up in the first words quoted above, "to make visible the community of mankind."

This doctrine, of course, was by no means new, at least in essence. But his application of the doctrine was novel. He was not content, as some have been, to define the goal of human endeavour and leave the way to it undefined. He knew that the mere ingemination of peace would do nothing to deliver the world from the woe of combat, and that ideals of love and brotherhood are not realised by making them the commonplaces of hortatory elocution. Would you "make visible the great community"? Then you must

TYPE OF A GOOD INTERNATIONAL BARGAIN

have, not moral inspiration only, but a definite technique and a scientific basis. Is collective security your ideal? Then you must equip your ideal with a business-like method and you must find trained, competent, expert and trustworthy agents for the application of it.

Nor is it necessary to invent a new method for the purpose, nor to conjure up a new type of man, nor to wait for a general reform of human morals. There are already in existence many types of community, many forms of human association, many varieties of incorporation, which provide their members with collective security on specified lines, which make contracts to that effect, and can be trusted to keep them. Which of them has the best claim to rest on a scientific basis? Which has the best record for trustworthiness? Which has proved itself most fertile in resource, most flexible in application, most rapid in extension, most triumphant in overcoming difficulties at first deemed insuperable. Which stands pre-eminent in creating a common interest out of interests which diverge and collide when acting in isolation? Which, in fine, has done most to convert the Christian precept "to bear one another's burdens" from a moral ideal floating in the upper air of pious dreams into a business-like undertaking resting on a scientific basis and visibly planted on the earth?

You will find what you are seeking, answered

Royce, in an institution, familiar to the economic world, which has solved, in its own field, the very problem which the internationalist would solve in his, that of giving the collective security of a powerful incorporation to each of its component units, themselves individually insecure, and does this, moreover, by exact methods of science and a highly developed technique. It is the institution know as Mutual Insurance.

Is there no possibility, then, of extending this beneficent and trustworthy mode of procedure from the narrower fields where it now works to the wider field of the international horizon? Would not a contract between nations framed on that model, or a series of such, be an effectual means to co-operation? And would it not offer, in virtue of its self-protecting technique, a security far more solid and likely to last than a political compact between nations standing one to another in the dangerous relation of armed units, liable at any moment to repudiate their pledges in a "passionate moment" or under the stress of emergency? Would it not inspire a firmer confidence?

That the idea of insurance is not altogether foreign in this connection is suggested by the arguments of various eminent persons who have lately been defending the increase of our own armaments as "a form of national insurance." The argument is attractive, but falls into absurdity when we reflect that if every nation proceeds to "insure" itself independently in this manner, as indeed most of them are now doing, a situation will be created in which *none* of them is insured, the position of each becoming progressively insecure the more the others insure themselves in this way—like a group of gamblers gathered round a table for a friendly game of cards, each "insured" against possible unfriendliness on the part of the others by a sufficient six-shooter in his hip-pocket. Our philosopher's idea of international insurance, as a means to collective security, can hardly be more impracticable than this.

The idea, unfortunately, was not fully worked out, the author's life being cut short before he could complete what he had begun. From the rough and tentative sketch he left behind it appears that he was far from recommending any sudden or wholesale application of his method. He would plant an acorn, not a full-grown oak. He would begin with any form of national risk which actuarial science, after thorough exploration of the matter, might declare to be internationally insurable. Of these he was convinced that more than one could be found among the many risks to life and fortune to which nations, as nations, are exposed.* His study of the history of

---

* Risks connected with the means of communication between nations (shipping, aircraft, cables, wireless, etc.) have been suggested as suitable for the beginning of international insurance. If war risks

insurance, so timid and circumscribed in its origin, so firm and penetrating in its present hold on social life, further convinced him that, a beginning once made in any international form, a rapid extension would follow; that with each new advance peacekeeping forces would be liberated and war-making forces tend to subside.

Whatever the form chosen for the beginning might be, it was to be backed by an adequate International Fund contributed by the nations after the manner of policy-holders, and administered by internationally chosen Trustees. Nor was this to be undertaken as a purely philanthropic enterprise. Following the lines of insurance as now practised, it was to make good business for the participating nations. Our philosopher was not of those who regard a profitable business enterprise as likely to be immoral. And to critics who declared that his international fund was impracticable his answer was, "not more impracticable than an international police"—an answer which reveals at a glance the broad significance of Royce's proposal. It lay in his judgment that an international *fund*, administered by trustworthy methods, was a more promising security for peace

---

are included, such as damage to life and property by air raids, coupled with the condition that an aggressor nation forfeited its own policy, the peacekeeping effect of the arrangement would be almost decisive. To start with, however, nothing so ambitious need be attempted.

than any form of international *force*, disposed of by an uncertain diplomacy and composed of elements whose cohesion in a crisis was more than doubtful.

Such is our philosopher's hint of a possible line of advance, starting from familiar ground and using a well-tried method, by which we might *begin* to make "the great community" visible on the earth, and begin in a business-like way. As a hint to creative thinking, it seems to deserve attention. It should also be of interest to those who believe that religion will have something to do in helping to solve the problem of collective security. It was the outcome of a profoundly religious philosophy.

"I still believe," writes our author in the last of his published essays, "that if insurance of the nations, for the nations, by the nations once appeared in a practicable form, it would thenceforward not vanish from the earth, but would tend, more than any international influence has yet tended, to make the community of mankind visible, and so to further gradually, perhaps slowly, the cause of peace. . . . At no point would any fundamental transformation of human nature be needed as a condition to its possessing a genuine, peacemaking potent influence. Once constituted . . . it would further increase both its direct working and its indirect furthering of the cause of humanity. It would stand in opposition to none of the other peacemaking influences. It might well tend in the long run to transform international relations."*

From the above summary it will be seen that what our author was aiming at, in this novel proposal of his, was the formation of a beneficent international *habit*, which might check and finally overcome the dangerous habit of warmaking, for such it largely is. In this he deserves credit for a sound psychology. Dangerous habits, whether of nations or individuals, are not to be overcome, as the practice of many would suggest they can be, by denouncing their wickedness, nor by proving their unreasonableness, nor even by calling for a change of heart in the name of religion, or a change of mind in the name of reason. Against these methods of direct attack, the power of habit, when firmly established, stands unshaken—a truth which moralists, propagandists and hortatory persons in general are somewhat slow to assimilate. It is the habit of habit, if such words may be used, to defy all arguments against it, and yield only to its own kind. It begins to weaken through the growth of another habit, contrary to that in possession, and dies out as the newcomer drains its energies—the method of indirect attack, which must often begin at a point far removed from the final

* *The Hope of the Great Community*, pp. 76 and 91; The Macmillan Company.

objective, and always requires much patience and business-like skill.

This interesting line of thought we shall endeavour, in the next two chapters, to carry a stage further. The essence of the matter lies in the suggestion that *fund* is a more suitable medium than *force* for international co-operation in a world economically conditioned. We are here in presence of a possible turning-point in the history of the League of Nations, the turning-point from co-operative *fighting* to co-operative *working*, from *Arms and the Man* to *Tools and the Man*—the birth of a new Epic.

In choosing fund rather than force as the medium of collective action we must not expect to escape from difficulties. But, whatever they may be, they will not be avoided by choosing force as the medium. The advocates of force have the double difficulty on their hands of (1) creating their force and (2) raising the funds to maintain it. Our own difficulties are of the second class only.

CHAPTER XIV

DISARMAMENT THE PRELUDE TO CO-OPERATION

"At the beginning of January, 1937, in a quarterly report of a German Bureau of Business Research, the world's total expenditure on armaments in 1936 amounted to 2,916 millions sterling, compared with 844 millions in 1913 and 1,444 millions in 1929."—F. W. HIRST, *Armaments*, p. 101.

"As I watch the figures mounting up, as I reflect upon the growing cost of the maintenance of this vast panoply when we have completed it, I cannot help being impressed by the incredible folly of civilisation."—MR. NEVILLE CHAMBERLAIN on January 29th, 1937.

"Stupidity, savage unreason, fitter for Bedlam than for a human world."—CARLYLE.

WE have often read in books of travel how the explorer, armed for self-protection or for hunting game, suddenly finds himself surrounded by threatening savages, and of how, wishing to indicate his peaceable intentions, our explorer, if he is a brave man, promptly lays down his arms and the angry natives, understanding the gesture, do likewise. Friendly relations are thus set on foot and the explorer hospitably entertained by those who, but an hour ago, were preparing to kill and eat him. Such is the first step on the road to peace, whether in Papua or in Europe.

Total and sudden disarmament is, of course, impossible; but until the nations have given evidence of the sincerity of their peaceable intentions by laying down at least some part of the arms they now brandish in each other's faces no progress whatsoever can be made on the road to durable peace. Even an agreement to reduce armaments by five per cent of their present strength would have great value in restoring confidence. It would begin to dissipate the atmosphere of conflict in which international policy has so long been conducted. And it would be a good bargain from every point of view. This is a precept of common sense and not a dogma of any creed, pacifist or otherwise.

To an observer from another sphere, unaccustomed to the mad doings of mankind, it would certainly seem a strange thing that a number of civilised nations armed to the teeth and bleeding themselves white to increase their armaments should nevertheless enter into a compact *not to use them*. These nations, he would say, cannot be in earnest when they profess the desire to live at peace one with another. Were they in earnest a far simpler mode of attaining their object would occur to them. They would lay down their arms, or at least begin to do so. Like the traveller among the Papuan savages, they would prove their peaceable intentions in that manner, and proceed to friendly co-operation from that point. Having agreed not to use their arms for mutual destruction, why, in heaven's name, he would ask, do they still retain and increase them as though for that very purpose? Clearly they are not in earnest and have no confidence in each other's good faith. What, then, is the value of their agreement? It will surely be broken as soon as any of them is driven by fear or ambition to break it. Such would be the reasonings and the questionings of an observer unacquainted with the fact that habit is more powerful than reason in the life of nations.

What would our comment be if we were to read in some book of nonsense of a Total Abstinence Society composed exclusively of brewers and distillers, each exerting himself to outdo the others in the production of beer and whisky? This, we should say, is a very bad joke. Yet what is the difference in principle between a Total Abstinence Society composed of competing brewers and distillers and a League for the prevention of war composed of nations competing in the race for armaments? The latter conception is the worst joke of the two. The tragedy of it overwhelms the comedy.

From all this we draw the conclusion that durable peace will not come even distantly into sight until a check is put on this "savage unreason." The nations agreed to check it under the terms of the Covenant eighteen years ago. But they promptly proceeded to break that agreement and have been breaking it ever since, until now they seem to have forgotten that they ever made it. Of all the breaches of the Covenant this,

DISARMAMENT THE PRELUDE TO CO-OPERATION

in which all the leading nations participated, has been the most serious and has done more than all the rest to reveal the scanty regard in which the sanctity of treaties is held by the parties. It has shown the nations how little they can depend on each other's good faith, and ruined the value of the Covenant as a peacekeeping instrument long before the crisis arose which put it to the test sixteen years later. Let it never be forgotten that the Conference which met at Geneva to deal with the default of Italy under Article XI was itself a Conference of defaulting nations under Article VIII. They had all defaulted in their obligation to disarm.* Better would it have been had they never agreed to do so. Such an agreement counts for nothing until it is fulfilled, and if unfulfilled, as this was, is obviously worse than nothing.

It is the deed, not the word, that counts. With the first check on the race for armaments, be the check never so slight, the process will begin which is to deliver the nations from the scourge of war. Peace will then be in sight and will gradually come into nearer view in proportion as more arms are laid down. The secret for the pacification of the world is no hidden mystery. It is an open secret.

* According to Mr. Francis W. Hirst (*Armaments*, pp. 84–5), the total expenditure of Great Britain on armaments in 1913–14 was £77,000,000. In 1934–35, before the Abyssinian crisis, it was £122,000,000. According to the same authority, it may approach £300,000,000 in 1937–8. So much for "the sanctity of treaties."

CHAPTER XV

DISARMAMENT AND ECONOMIC CO-OPERATION LINKED TOGETHER

IF the sovereign states of the world are taken one by one it is obvious that each is intent on self-preservation. But if we view them collectively it would seem that some "power not themselves" is goading them on to self-destruction. The tendency of the whole seems to be in opposition to the tendencies of the parts; as though a Suicide Club were to be composed of members each determined to preserve his own life at all costs. In correspondence to this we should observe, on studying their mentality, that each of them desires to live in peace, while the totality seems afflicted with a war-complex which overpowers their individual desires for peace and drives them continually in the direction of war. *Sauve qui peut* is the principle on which each is acting; the result in the total is a general rush down a steep place into the sea—in other words, the race for armaments. Individually they appear to be sane, but collectively mad.

Were this curious phenomenon referred to a psychologist for explanation he would probably point to the war-complex as the key. He would remind us that these nations have brooded on war so long, had the image of it so continually before their minds, kept the discussion of it so prominent in the forefront of their common deliberations and, finally, become so obsessed with the fear of it, that their collective behaviour has become that of a panic-stricken crowd. Asked for a remedy, his reply would necessarily be of a general character. He would tell us that the only way to deal with such a case is to create *a powerful diversion*. "If by any means," he would say, "you can turn the minds of these infatuated masses in a new direction, draw their attention off to another object, and get them busy together in the pursuit of some common interest, you will have taken the only possible way to break the power of their war-complex and bring them back to reason and common sense."

In this chapter we shall try to follow the psychologist's hint. Our search will be for that "powerful diversion" recommended by him as the antidote to the war-complex, and we shall endeavour to give the idea what precision we can. This search might have been undertaken, and perhaps one day will be, by the League of Nations. But, unfortunately, the League of Nations, instead of liberating the corporate mentality from the war-complex, as many hoped it would do, fell unwittingly into its power.

CO-OPERATION OR COERCION?

Our starting-point will be the assurance recently given by leading members of His Majesty's Government that they and their colleagues are prepared to do all in their power to further the attainment of two objects: (1) all-round limitation of armaments, and (2) economic co-operation on an international basis. Our suggestion will be that if these two objects, instead of being pursued in separation, can be so linked together that the pursuit of them becomes *a joint operation*, we shall be on the way to a "powerful diversion" of the international mind from its present disastrous preoccupation with the image and vocabulary of war.

Agreements between nations are most likely to be kept when they are pitched on ground where the temptations to bad faith are relatively low and the inducements to good relatively high. In both respects economic agreements compare favourably with those of the military or coercionist type, which always involve the risk that one or more of the parties may be dragged into war against its will. Not that economic agreements are completely immune from infraction through weakness or treachery. No human compact can ever be that, so long, at least, as original sin is unexpunged from human nature. But they can be so contrived as to be good business for the parties. In that form, though not invulnerable to bad faith, they are less vulnerable to it than agreements that point forward to co-operative fighting.

An international *fund* would be more likely to function according to plan and follow the rules laid down for its administration than an international *force* to obey orders, act loyally in concert, and strike promptly without dissension at any point where its services might be required. If the nations want to pool anything for their common protection, their economic resources seem to be the most suitable for the purpose; far more suitable, certainly, than their fighting powers. The pooling of the latter would inevitably bring on a collision with the principle of national sovereignty on every occasion when the question arose of using the common force in war, since the decision to go to war is one which no sovereign state can pass on to another authority, at Geneva or anywhere else.

Where the use of a common fund is concerned, this difficulty is less formidable, and at the minimum in the case of a good bargain. Whence we may draw the conclusion that if international co-operation is to be set on foot in a form which gives reasonable hope that it will not be wrecked by bad faith, the military or coercive form should be avoided and a beginning made on economic ground. An international fund is far more manageable than an international force.

Here our search for a "powerful diversion" encounters a most formidable obstacle. It lies in the comprehensive character of the race for armaments, in the vast variety of forces that contribute to its momentum. War machinery, whether for attack or defence, has now become so closely interlocked with economic machinery, both financial and industrial, that a check on the one is necessarily a check on the other, a diversion of either necessarily a diversion of both. The raising of the enormous sums now spent on armaments would clearly be impossible were it not that the war machinery and the financial machinery of a nation work together as an indivisible system.

The connection is still more clearly seen when we consider the nature of modern armaments. The armament industry, needless to say, is not carried on exclusively in the factories where cannon, rifles, explosives, and the other munitions are produced. A vast congregation of industries is drawn into the net—iron, coal, oil, transport, chemicals, machinery, and innumerable others, all "mobilised" to make their respective contributions. Not to enlarge unnecessarily on the obvious, suffice it to say that a reduction of armament expenditure in any country, if unaccompanied by countervailing measures, would be followed immediately by economic disturbance, involving a general increase of unemployment and an extensive lowering of quotations on every Stock Exchange.

To stop the race for armaments is by no means the simple operation suggested by the mere words.

It would be stopping a race in which all the main currents of finance and industry are deeply involved, and in which the bulk of the working population are not spectators merely but participants. When once the industry of the nation has been "mobilised for defence," as high authorities have recently urged it must be, it will be found extremely difficult to demobilise later on and to remobilise for anything else. Getting into the race for armaments is much easier than getting out of it.

Precisely at this point, where the prospect seems darkest, the light begins to dawn. Bearing in mind that war machinery and economic machinery are inseparably one, does it not follow that the limitation of armaments and economic co-operation must be linked together as a joint operation if either is to be attempted with any hope of success? May it not be that here is an opportunity for the countervailing measures which are needed to offset the checks to industry involved in limitation, reduce the shock to a minimum, and absorb whatever shock there may be? What if limitation of armaments, which by itself is purely negative, were made an integral part of a positive scheme for liberating the channels of international trade, now extensively frozen and blocked, and so bringing to industry a greater and more lasting prosperity than the temporary prosperity it now gets from the pouring out of colossal sums on the production of armaments? What if the two operations, each impossible in isolation from the other, were so combined that the one would furnish the means for setting the other on foot, thereby converting it from a vague aspiration into a business-like enterprise profitable to all the parties? As we ponder these questions there emerges the dim outline of a good bargain.

This bargain may be imagined as taking shape somewhat as follows. We conceive that a conference has been summoned (this is inevitable) for considering the limitation of armaments; but with this important difference from its ill-starred predecessor, that limitation is now to be considered as linked to economic co-operation, and not as an isolated question. Avoiding the confused, complicated and virtually insoluble problems on which the predecessor broke down, the proposal will be made to apply limitation, not to armaments *per se*, but, far more simply, to the colossal *expenditure* they now involve, probably £2,000,000,000 per annum in Europe alone—attacking the enemy, so to speak, at the source of his supplies.

With this twofold object in view the parties would agree (1) to follow the recent suggestion of the French Government by publishing their budgetary expenditure on armaments, and (2) to reduce that expenditure in a specified proportion all round—for the sake of argument, say 10 per cent; the 10 per cent so saved from expenditure on mutual destruction to be contributed by each of the consenting nations to an International Fund, deposited in the Bank of International Settlements, and used for promoting and financing economic co-operation on definite lines. With the two objects thus linked together, and our conference discussing them in that form, the outlines of a good bargain become fairly clear.

At the present rate of expenditure on armaments the pool in three years would conceivably amount to £600,000,000; but, even if we reduce that by half, the means would be created for giving reality to economic co-operation in forms which, under competent management, would have profitable results to all the participants. We may conceive the Fund as controlled and managed by a Board of International Trustees, working under rules of equity devised in form and supervised in operation by the League of Nations, now equipped with a powerful instrument of constructive peace.

As to the possible modes of employing the Fund, five can be named at once, each pointing the way to others of like nature: (1) the stabilisation of currencies with a view to freeing the frozen currents of international trade; (2) the lowering of tariffs for the same purpose; (3) financing the distribution of raw materials by means of appropriate credits; (4) promoting international social services of the kind now carried on, but cramped for lack of funds, by the League; (5) the assistance of nations afflicted by natural calamities such as earthquakes, famine and flood. These five and doubtless many others. The position of the contributory nations would be analogous to that of policy-holders in an Insurance Company. What each got out of the Fund would be proportional to what it put in.

No addition would be made to the present burden of taxation in any country. The operation would consist simply in the transference of so much national revenue from unproductive to productive use—so much withdrawn from the service of the war-machine, and converted to the service of constructive peace, so much from *Arms and the Man* to *Tools and the Man*.

Of all this only a rough sketch, such as a man might draw in the sand with the point of his stick, can here be attempted. Enough if the principle of the "joint operation" has been made clear. The moral level is that of a good bargain, which, if it is not the highest level, is certainly not the lowest. The appeal is to common sense, humblest among the servants of the moral ideal, but perhaps the most trustworthy. Its merits, if any, are comparative. If judged fantastic, the answer must be that it can hardly be more fantastic than the coercionist plan, hitherto in the ascendant, on which so much high talent has been wasted. There seems, however, to be this in its favour, that if once set on foot, even on a limited scale, its tendency would be to expand and to draw into itself more and more of the forces now making for catastrophe. Its action would be progressive. A self-developing common interest would be established on a business-like foundation. Thus the nations would be hopefully started on the way to that "powerful diversion" which our psychologist rightly indicated as the sole remedy for their collective madness. Those who regard the sudden advent of world peace as impossible and are content to work for the gradual development of collective security may see here a finger-post pointing to a line of action not unworthy of further exploration.

There is at all events one important consideration of which the advocates of economic co-operation on the international scale do not appear to have taken sufficient account. This is the necessity of financing it with adequate capital. Perhaps they have been a little afraid of the word "capital" as likely to rouse opposition in certain quarters, notably in the socialist or communist sections of the community, though there is no reason why either of these denominations should object to capital when placed under international control. Be that as it may, it is obvious that whatever form the co-operative project might take it will be found, as soon as we get to actual business, that the project would be unworkable unless furnished with adequate funds, that is to say, with capital. Were the stabilisation of currencies, for example, to be undertaken on the international scale, the creation of an international fund, similar to that behind the existing tripartite arrangement, but much vaster in amount, would be the first necessity. And so with any of the other forms we have named or with any, indeed, that we have not named. *Economic co-operation on the international scale is impossible without international capital.*

Our suggestion provides for this. It converts unproductive expenditure on armaments (a modest portion of it) into productive capital for the financing of economic co-operation in any form deemed wise to undertake. Gradual disarmament and economic co-operation are thus linked together into a single process.

CHAPTER XVI

HOW TWO GREAT NATIONS CAME TO BURY THE HATCHET

OUR argument will be found to agree at one essential point with the doctrine of extreme pacifism, and yet to differ from it at another point equally essential. Like the pacifists, we believe that the first step to peace and reconciliation is indicated by the formula "lay down your arms." But, unlike the pacifist, we address our formula not to our own nation, nor to any other, but to the *League of Nations in its corporate character*. To the nations taken one by one, our own among them, we say "be armed if you will." To the *League* of Nations we say "will to be unarmed." Let the League practise what it preaches—the doctrine of peace. Instead of binding the nations one by one to renounce war as the instrument of *their* policy, let it renounce war as an instrument of *its own* policy. Let it pursue its mission and go about its business *unarmed*. Is there any example to be set, any principle to be established, any lesson to be taught by the existence in the world of a great and powerful community which can do its work and achieve its purposes without invoking the support of the devil's instruments? Let the League of Nations be that community, set that example, establish that principle and teach that lesson. Let *the whole* will to go unarmed, and the time will not be long before the *parts*, left free to arm if they will, begin to see the wisdom of following suit. Disarmament, we repeat, is the key to the problem of peace, and the beginning of its use lies with the League of Nations. Unarmed, there is hope that the League may succeed at last in banishing war from the face of the earth. Armed, it is bound to fail.

At present the League has, fortunately, no arms of its own to lay down. But it has a constitution which unwisely commits it to use them under certain circumstances—an exasperating and war-provoking apparatus of "sanctions" which could only be worked, and with doubtful results even then, if the League were equipped with an armament "sufficient to deter the most powerful aggressor." Let it, then, lay down *all that*. Having no arms as yet, let it divest itself once and for all of the desire to possess them and of the proposal to create them. The way will then be opened for the fulfilment of its mission undisturbed by war-making preoccupations.

So far we have not advanced beyond the negative statement that the operations of our New Model will be unprotected by the devil's instruments—the proper name for the methods and weapons of modern warfare.* By what, then, will they be protected?

They will be protected, first, by the mutual and obvious advantages which good economic bargains offer to the parties concerned in them; and, second, by certain habits and traditions of good faith, lacking in the region of military commitments, but fairly well established in the economic sphere. Such protection, indeed, we do not regard as infallible. But we do regard it as vastly less fallible than the protection afforded by the bad bargains concealed under the phrase "a collective preponderance of strength," and set up in a field where good faith is notoriously lacking—vastly less fallible than *that* and, in the last resort, the only protection available for compacts between sovereign states. We think, moreover, that the guardianship of good faith would be enormously strengthened, though never to the point of infallibility, if all the covenanting parties were to declare openly and explicitly that they rely, and propose to rely, on nothing else. Were it not wiser to recognise this at the outset than to be forced by new disasters to the discovery that coercion is here impossible? To which procedure will sovereign states respond more favourably—a challenge to their good faith or a threat of sanctions? To which would you or I? Would you combine the two?

* A point to be remembered by those who talk loosely of "force," or romantically of the Christian man's duty to draw the "sword" in a righteous cause.

But do you not perceive how the one spoils the other—how the threat of sanctions assumes the possible *bad* faith of those on whose *good* faith you propose to rely?

That we are here on the right line seems to be confirmed by the following story of how two great nations, once bitter enemies, came to bury the hatchet.

At the present moment the firmest of Great Britain's allies and the best of her friends in Europe is France. But that friendship is of comparatively recent date. For many centuries, as we all know, a blood feud existed between the two countries and gave rise to repeated, protracted and ruinous wars. How was the change from enmity to friendship brought about? The question is well worth study by those who would see existing enmities similarly changed.

The change began in 1859, at the very time when Great Britain and France, as it so happened, were on the brink of war, and this country in a state of panic, the third of the kind during the space of little more than fifty years.* Those who would read the story in full will find it well told in Mr. Francis Hirst's admirable study of the present armament race, recently published and appropriately bound in black.† In the following

---

* *Three Panics*, by Richard Cobden.

† *Armaments: the Race and the Crisis*, by Francis W. Hirst. London: Cobden-Sanderson.

paragraphs we bring together a selection of the relevant passages,* separated in Mr. Hirst's account (pages 15 to 27) but here given continuously.

"When peace was restored in 1859 after the Indian Mutiny panic-mongers in the British press endeavoured to create a new alarm by exaggerated accounts of French naval preparations and by giving out that the French Admiralty had been spending enormous sums on shipbuilding. In both the House of Commons and the House of Lords public men asserted that a French invasion was imminent. Lord Palmerston insisted upon a fortification loan and a considerable addition to naval and military expenditure. Rifle corps were started all over the country and a volunteer force brought into existence. From forty-five thousand before the Crimean war the number of seamen was raised to eighty-five thousand and naval expenditure from six to thirteen millions. Napoleon's success [in the campaign against Austria] had given rise to the notion that his next adventure would be a descent on our coasts. This alarm caused the third, the last and the most serious of the French invasion panics.

"It was laid to rest partly by reason and ridicule but mainly by a great commercial treaty. It subsided through a diversion which created a peaceful psychology among the industrial and commercial classes.

* With Mr. Hirst's kind permission.

"In September 1859 Cobden visited Gladstone at Hawarden and they discussed the possibility of a commercial treaty with France [particulars in *Morley's Life of Gladstone*, book 5, chapter 2]. Gladstone seized the idea. It was arranged that Cobden should communicate with Napoleon and his ministers and work out with them a treaty that 'should open the way to a great fiscal reform and produce a solid and sterling pacification feeling.' But neither in Gladstone's nor Cobden's mind were economic reasons predominant. They were inspired by high moral and political considerations—to avert the threatened war with France, to arrest the wasteful and menacing competition in armaments and to promote international good will."

Gladstone's memorandum on the transaction runs as follows:

"A French panic prevailed, as strong as any of the other panics that have done so much discredit to this country. For this panic the treaty of commerce with France was the only sedative. It was, in fact, a counter-irritant; it aroused the sense of commercial interest to counteract the war passion. It was, and is, my opinion that the choice lay between the Cobden Treaty and, not the certainty, but the high probability, of a war with France."

Thus was the old blood feud brought to an end and the foundations laid for a lasting friendship between the two countries. How easy it would be to rewrite the whole story in terms appropriate to present conditions—to rewrite it and, perhaps, to enact it!

We commend the study of this story for the wider bearings it has on the main problem the League of Nations was created to solve and on the future of the League itself. Consider the outstanding features of it. Observe, in general, how the Gordian knot of a warlike entanglement was boldly cut through by a stroke of the economic sword. Observe, next, how the enemy was appeased by offering him a good bargain profitable to both sides, and how the effect of this in the two countries was to dissipate the atmosphere of conflict and divert the public mind from a war psychology to a peace psychology. Reflect especially on the word "diversion" used by Mr. Hirst and on "counter-irritant" used by Mr. Gladstone; and then consider the opportunity now awaiting the League to create a similar diversion, or counter-irritant, on a far vaster scale. Here, surely, was statesmanship of a very high order. Viewed in the light of that day and generation was it not a master-stroke, a highly effective combination of ideal aims with a business-like method? What a hint for the League, bent, as its orthodox supporters say it is, on "the prevention of war!"

CHAPTER XVII

AN HISTORICAL PARALLEL FROM THE UNITED STATES

IN a letter to *The Times* of July 8th, 1936, Dr. Nicholas Murray Butler appealed for a close study of the problem now confronting the League of Nations in the light of the parallel problem successfully solved by the statesmen who drew up the constitution of the United States. We say "successfully," for not only did the measures taken succeed in combining the original thirteen states, by no means on good terms with one another at the time, into a Federal Union, but they made possible the entry into the Union of a succession of others, thirty-five in number, whose existence at the time was not dreamed of, and to the gradual growth of the whole into the vast totality of the present United States. This building-up of a community of states on the American continent, conscious of a common interest and loyal to it, wears an obvious resemblance to the task the League of Nations, as its name implies, was founded to achieve on a greater scale. Though the resemblance of the American achievement to the task before the League does not amount to identity, it holds at certain essential points, and

AN HISTORICAL PARALLEL FROM THE UNITED STATES

a study of the principles underlying it can hardly fail to throw light on the matters discussed in this book. We propose, therefore, to follow Dr. Butler's advice, referring in particular to the work of a great statesman, one of the greatest, in laying the foundations of the United States—Alexander Hamilton.*

When the American statesmen of 1787 were engaged in the very difficult task of combining the thirteen quarrelsome American states into a Federal Union or League, they were confronted with a proposal to introduce into the constitution a minatory clause analogous to Article XVI of the Covenant, a clause assuming possible bad faith on the part of a signatory state, and threatening the delinquent with coercion by an armed combination of the others—the many against the one. This proposal was hotly debated and, in the upshot, decisively rejected. It was described by Alexander Hamilton as "one of the maddest projects that was ever devised," and by others in similar terms. He argued that the Union, if it were to last, must

---

* Alexander Hamilton (1757–1804) was born in the island of Nevis in the West Indies. His father was of Scottish descent, his mother descended from a family of French protestants. He began life as an apprentice in a sugar merchant's store, afterwards went to college in New York, became Washington's chief aide-de-camp during the War of Independence and Secretary of the Treasury in Washington's administration. At the age of thirty he played a leading part in framing the Constitution and securing its acceptance by the states. He was mortally wounded in a duel with Aaron Burr. A masterly study of the life and work of this remarkable man, and of the great events he helped to shape, will be found in *Alexander Hamilton*, by Frederick Scott Oliver (1906: new edition, 1931. Macmillan, 39th thousand).

be *non-coercive* as between itself and the individual states composing it, that conflict and disruption would inevitably follow if the coercive basis were adopted. The subsequent history of the United States seems to prove his wisdom.

The reasons which led to the triumph of the anti-coercionist policy at that critical moment in history are so pertinent to the international conditions of the present day that the matter seems worthy of further elaboration.

The parallel between the American problem of 1787 and the League problem of to-day is, of course, not complete. It may be well, therefore, to note the difference before stressing the resemblance.

1. The thirteen states to be united into a political league shared in varying degree the same political traditions; the inhabitants were largely of one race and spoke the same language.

2. They had recently been united, though sometimes half-heartedly and not without loyalist opposition, in resistance to the British Crown; and they had all shared in the victory. There was no question, therefore, of bringing defeated states into the Union.

3. Whatever their mutual animosities may have been, they lacked the bitterness and tenacity of the age-long feuds of Europe and were of lesser intensity than the ill will engendered by the Treaty of Versailles.

4. Unlike the great states of the modern world, they were not armed or arming to the teeth for unknown purposes and, in consequence, the fear of war as a psychological factor in the negotiations, though present in a degree, had not acquired the dominating influence to which it has been brought by the enormous armaments of to-day and by modern methods of warfare. Exhausted by their recent struggle with the British, not even the strongest of them was very formidable.

5. The question at issue did not take the form of putting a final end to war in the world at large, nor even of finding an *infallible* method of preventing war as between the thirteen negotiating states. "If they want to fight," said Ellsworth, "they may do it, and no frame of government can possibly prevent it." (Subsequently they did fight, North against South.)

6. In forming the American Union two objects were aimed at and successfully accomplished, of which only the first is attempted by the League of Nations: (1) the union of the thirteen independent states into a political League; (2) the fusion of the inhabitants of those states into a single nation with a single government and electoral control over its machinery. By attaining the second of these objects along with the first the people of the United States were given the power of dismissal and impeachment over elected public servants

who might "disregard their obligations" under the constitution. In this way the whole was brought under the sovereignty of a united people, and the question *quis custodiet custodes* was, to that extent, answered. There is no united people behind the League of Nations who could dismiss or impeach its executive for a breach of the constitution.

Two rival plans were brought forward for discussion at the Philadelphia Convention: "the New Jersey Plan" and "the Virginia Plan." The New Jersey, or "Federalist," Plan would have united the states into a political league, but failed to unite their inhabitants into a single people under a single government. The Virginia, or "Nationalist," Plan would have united the inhabitants of the states into a single people, but destroyed the independence of the separate states, or impaired it to such a degree as to make a political league impossible. As originally drafted both plans involved the principle of collective coercion of the parts by the whole. This was eliminated, and the result was a compromise between the two with the Virginia Plan as the basis.

Other differences might be named, but the above are sufficient to warn us against stressing the parallel too hard.

Nevertheless there were quarrelsome forces at work in these states which would certainly have led to internecine war had they been allowed to

AN HISTORICAL PARALLEL FROM THE UNITED STATES

develop, and were only with difficulty restrained from breaking out. On the whole the relationships of the states one to another were sufficiently hostile and dangerous to make the problem of their political union exceedingly difficult. There was open rebellion in Massachusetts, where Washington was mobbed; Virginia was hated by the northern states; New York and Connecticut were at daggers drawn; tariff walls were erected between the two and between others; new sources of discord were developing with the migration of the people towards the West. Each state had its own constitution and Legislature; each had its own militia; each insisted on its rights as free and sovereign within its own borders, and any attempt to impair this sovereignty, or to establish the domination of the stronger states over the weaker—and the inequalities were great—would have been the signal for instant strife. To British observers at the time, though they were doubtless prejudiced, it seemed impossible to evoke order out of such a chaos, and the break-up of the Union was freely predicted both then and for a long time afterwards. In a Memorandum submitted to the Paris Conference of 1919 by the American Peace Society the situation is thus described:

"The thirteen free sovereign independent states of that day were confronted with debt, commercial rivalries, inefficiencies, inequalities, separate treaties, violations of contracts, depreciated currency, varieties of opinion and practice, rebellion; in short, international anarchy . . . The American states set themselves the task of overcoming these difficulties."

Mr. F. S. Oliver, in his admirable study of Hamilton, after describing the refusal of the individual states to part with "one shred" of their sovereignty, continues as follows:*

"The thirteen states proceeded to indulge themselves in the costly luxury of an internecine tariff war. The states with seaports preyed upon their landlocked brethren and provoked a boycott in return. Pennsylvania attacked Delaware. Connecticut was oppressed by Rhode Island and New York. New Jersey, lying between New York and Pennsylvania, was compared to a 'cask tapped at both ends'; North Carolina, between South Carolina and Virginia, to 'a patient bleeding at both stumps.' It was a dangerous game, ruinous in itself and, behind the custom-house officers, men were beginning to furbish up the locks of their muskets. . . . At one time war between Vermont, New Hampshire and New York seemed all but inevitable."

It is not surprising that the American leaders were by no means of one mind in their efforts to evoke an ordered government out of the prevailing anarchy. There was ardent controversy, sustained on both sides by well-equipped protagonists. To

*Alexander Hamilton, pp. 134-135.

the one side it seemed obvious that without coercion, implemented by what would now be called "a collective preponderance of strength," the anarchic elements would never be permanently kept in order. To the other side, which ultimately triumphed, it seemed equally obvious that armed coercion or the threat of it, as applied by the Union to any particular state, would be fatal to the end in view.

Here it is that we may find, in spite of the differences named above, an illuminating parallel to the problem now confronting the League of Nations, and perhaps an object-lesson. A closer examination of the controversy, in which Hamilton showed a far-sighted statesmanship, will make this apparent.

Then, precisely as now, the problem was to form a League or Union on lines that would render it unlikely to break up through the default or rebellion of particular states, all of them equally hard set in the assertion of its individual sovereignty as "free and independent." Was this object to be attained by *force*, that is, by the armed combination of loyal states against any particular state which might break its pledge to abide by the terms of the Union? Or could it be attained otherwise? Then, as now, controversy centred on the word "force" or, as we say, "sanctions." What part was forcible coercion to play in maintaining the Union and ensuring the loyalty of member-states to their obligations under the Constitution? On the one side were those who maintained, just as many supporters of the League maintain to-day, that the Union would be powerless unless it commanded a collective preponderance of strength and were constitutionally empowered to use it for the coercion of a defaulter or a breaker of the peace. Had their counsels prevailed the Constitution of the United States would have contained a provision identical in principle with Articles X and XVI of the Covenant. "The Virginia Plan" laid before the Philadelphia Convention on May 29th, 1787, contained as originally drafted, the following provision: "To call forth the forces of the Union against any member of the Union failing to fulfil its duty under the Articles thereof."*

This proposal was met by the argument that sovereign political states (and this, it must be remembered, is what the American states claimed to be) are not coercible except by actual war, and that any coercive provision introduced into the Constitution would inevitably provoke the very strife it was intended to prevent. Force, it was admitted, is indispensable to civil government for the preservation of law and order, but only as employed by the state *against individuals*. As an

* For this and for most of the quotations which follow we are indebted to an admirable article by Arthur D. Call on "Force and World Peace" in *World Affairs*, June 1936, since reprinted by the American Peace Society, Washington, D.C.

instrument of coercion applied to sovereign states it is only another name for war, no matter whether the application of it be collective or otherwise, while the threat of it is nothing else than a declaration of war made in advance of the contingency it is intended to prevent. Against such a provision (here we should think of Articles X and XVI) all "free, sovereign and independent States" are antecedently in rebellion and are certain to rebel, if they are powerful enough, the moment coercion is applied or even threatened, the maintenance of their independence requiring nothing less, while, at the same time, they acquire a new justification for their rebellious conduct. And not only is the sovereign state non-coercible (except by defeat in war), but further, it will refuse when called upon to take part in coercing another state, whenever such coercion would involve the surrender of sovereign control over its own forces into the hands of collective authority. Such were Alexander Hamilton's objections to the principle of coercion. "It is one of the maddest projects that was ever devised," he writes in the *Federalist*. "Can we believe," he goes on, "that a [sovereign] State will ever suffer itself to be used as an instrument of coercion? The thing is a dream. It is impossible."

Further statements by Hamilton to the same effect are as follows. Addressing the Convention on June 18th, 1787, he said:

"A certain portion of military force is absolutely necessary in large communities . . . but how can this force be exerted on the State? It is impossible. It amounts to a war between the parties."

In the following year he writes to the *Federalist:*

"Whoever considers the populousness and strength of the States singly at the present juncture, and looks forward to what they will become, even at the distance of half a century, will at once dismiss as idle and visionary any scheme which aims at regulating their movements by laws to operate upon them in their collective capacities and to be executed by a coercion applicable to them in the same capacities. . . . Even in those Confederacies composed of members smaller than many of our counties, the principle of legislation for sovereign States, supported by military coercion, has never been found effectual. . . . In most instances attempts to coerce the refractory and disobedient [States] have been the signal of bloody war, in which one half of the Confederacy has displayed its banners against the other half."

James Madison expresses himself in similar terms. In the Session* of May 31st, 1787, he said:

"A Union of States containing such an ingredient provides for its own destruction. The use of force against a State would look more like a declaration of war than an infliction of punishment and would probably be considered by the

* Of the Philadelphia Convention.

party attacked as a dissolution of all previous compacts by which it might be bound."

Oliver Ellsworth, later Chief Justice of the Supreme Court, takes up the same point in his address to the Convention of Connecticut.

"A necessary consequence of the principle of coercion by arms is a war of the States one against the other. . . . This Constitution does not attempt to coerce sovereign bodies, States, in their political capacity. No coercion is applicable to such bodies, but that of an armed force. I am for that coercion which acts only on delinquent individuals."

From these quotations it is clear that the problem facing the American statesmen of 1787 was that of combining a number of sovereign states into a Union, Confederation or League, but in such a way as to leave intact the sovereignty claimed by each. To achieve this double and apparently paradoxical object, it was resolved that no coercive provisions, no sanctions, nothing that would have corresponded to Articles X and XVI in the Covenant, should have place in the Compact. And this for two reasons: (1) that such provisions would inevitably become a source of conflict between the covenanting states; (2) that in any case they would be futile since, as Ellsworth said, "if the United States and the individual States will quarrel, if they want to fight, no frame of government can possibly prevent it." From the nature of the case the threat would fail to materialise whenever an occasion arose for putting it into operation. The best that could be done, therefore, to ensure continued peace within the group was so to frame the Union as to reduce to a minimum the likelihood of their "wanting to quarrel." The introduction of coercive provisions, far from reducing the likelihood of conflict to a minimum, would have the contrary effect of raising it to a maximum. As constabulary business the coercion of a delinquent state by the Union was impossible; nothing short of war could make it effective. For these reasons it would be "one of the maddest projects that was ever devised."

The fact that, in spite of these principles, civil war actually broke out in the Union three-quarters of a century later, should be viewed in the light of Ellsworth's saying: "If these States want to fight, no frame of government can possibly prevent it." The saying is equally applicable to a League of Nations of any conceivable form or constitution. There is no infallible method of preventing armed and sovereign states from rebelling against the League of which they are members, or from fighting one another—*if they want to*. But there are methods of reducing the risk. A League of European or other nations so devised that it would last three-quarters of a century without a disruptive quarrel, as the

AN HISTORICAL PARALLEL FROM THE UNITED STATES

United States lasted, would certainly do well, and would probably last longer, with promise of yet further continuance. The coercive League of 1919 lasted sixteen years (with notable secessions meanwhile) and broke down, as Hamilton would have predicted, on the first attempt to apply coercion to a powerful rebel. To avert a European war, coercion had to be abandoned.

At this point there comes into view a further difference, in addition to those named above, between the American problem of 1787 and the League problem of to-day. Controversy between the coercionists and the non-coercionists of 1787 was not confused, as it now is, by the distinction between economic and military coercion under the name of sanctions.* How Hamilton would have viewed the distinction is not open to doubt. He would have pointed out that the resort to economic sanctions would only serve to delay the discovery, by the Union imposing them, that a sovereign state can be coerced only in the one way named above—by defeating it on the battlefield. Pressed beyond the point where they are merely harassing, they end in the bloodshed for which their pacifist supporters believe them a substitute. They point towards war and lead to it, like the first acts of a tragedy which reveal their tendencies to the death and destruction of the final act. They

* One might add further that the word "sanctions" (a wolf in sheep's clothing) had not yet come into diplomatic use as a means of giving a moral colour, or, at least, a politer sound, to "coercion."

point also to a coming split in the ranks of the coercionists or, as Hamilton would say, to "one half of the Confederacy displaying its banners against the other half."

From first to last of the long and bitter controversy over the form of the American Constitution Hamilton, while changing his opinion at other points, never lost sight of the essential fact, as the coercionist statesmen of our day seem to have done, that the threat of coercion, collective or otherwise, when addressed to a sovereign state, *is a threat to its sovereignty*, to its right to be sole master in its own house. He saw that the effect of coercion on a sovereign state, armed for the maintenance of its sovereignty, could be nothing else than to challenge and provoke it to armed resistance to the uttermost of its power. He saw further that each of the coercing states would realise that in thus threatening the sovereignty of another it was exposing its own sovereignty to similar encroachment on occasion given. Of this the effect would be to make the process of coercion lukewarm, dilatory, reluctant and, in the upshot, to ensure its breakdown—the point of Hamilton's question: "Can we believe that a sovereign state will ever suffer itself to be used as an instrument of coercion?"

Applying the argument to present conditions, it evidently requires that each European state, before embarking on the policy of collective coercion, should consider the effect of it *if applied to itself*. Can there be a doubt, for example, that Great Britain, if threatened with coercion from any source, would resist it to the uttermost? Can there be a doubt that her armaments would then be used, not for contributing to collective coercion, but for resisting it? What reason have we to believe that the reaction of other states would be more submissive?

In all this, it will be observed, Hamilton does not deny the necessity of coercion for the regulation of human affairs. Nor was he engaged, after the manner of modern pacifists, in a crusade for the abolition of war. He was not opposed to war-making as such. What Hamilton opposed and dismissed as impossible was a *coercive union* of states endowed, under the terms of the union, with the right to make war *on one or any of its own members*, and armed with a collective preponderance of strength for that purpose. Such a union, he argued, would be a contradiction not only in logic but in fact. It would contain the seed of internal conflict and be no union at all.

In keeping with this, and indeed another aspect of it, were Hamilton's views on the right of a government to engage the nation it ruled over in altruistic war on behalf of interests not its own. A government, he argued, has no such right and would place itself in the position of a defaulting trustee by embarking upon such warfare. His views on this matter are summarised by Mr. Oliver as follows:

"It was impossible, in Hamilton's view, for a nation to act towards other nations as a man of warm feelings would act towards his neighbours. A nation cannot afford to indulge itself in hatred or affection, magnanimity or revenge. In deciding upon its course of action, sentiment is as irrelevant a consideration as malice, and wars of chivalry are as iniquitous as wars of religion. The statesman who bends to an emotional outburst of public opinion as richly deserves to be shot as a general who surrenders a city out of compassion for the inhabitants. The stern test of the righteousness of a war is the permanent security of the State. A government which goes knight-erranting out of sympathy for foreign nations is like a trustee who subscribes to charities out of the property he has undertaken to administer.* A government, like a trustee, is responsible for the estate. . . . Pity and prejudice are equally out of place when ministers, in whom King or people has placed the serious confidence of decision, come to determine the tremendous issues of alliances and wars."†

Such were the principles that triumphed in forming the union of thirteen weak, quarrelsome

---

* With this we may compare Gladstone's words in 1869: "Is England so uplifted in strength that she can with prudence advertise herself as ready to undertake the general redress of wrongs?"

† *Alexander Hamilton*, p. 351.

and disordered states in 1787, a union which has survived and promises to survive on the scale and with the results we now see.

Are these principles applicable to the questions confronting us to-day? If coercion was a mad project then, has it become a sane project now? Is the principle of national sovereignty less deeply rooted among the nations of the modern world than it was among those thirteen states? And does the fact that most of these nations are armed to the teeth, each in the determination to be sole master of its own destiny (and none more determined than the British), render them more or less amenable to coercion? Is it less true to-day than it was then that "if these States will quarrel and want to fight no frame of government can possibly prevent it?" To be sure, the vast armaments now existing, if thrown into a common pool, would be so formidable that no dog would dare to bark in its presence. But where is the sovereign political state, determined to be master of its own destiny,* which shows the slightest disposition to let the control of its armed forces pass out of its own hands by throwing them into a pool at the disposal of a central authority? Would not such an arrangement involve the surrender, by each of the contributing states, wholly or in part, of the power intended to make

---

* "France," said M. Laval in his last speech to the Chamber, "will remain mistress of her own destiny." Mr. Baldwin might have replied: "So will the British Empire."

it master of its own destiny? Imagine the British Fleet taking its orders from Geneva!

These questions may all be summed up into one. Are the difficulties of union among the European states to-day, hard set in the assertion of national sovereignty, and armed to the teeth for asserting it, greater, on the whole, than those successfully overcome by the American statesmen of 1787? The answer is—*they are immensely greater for those who would base the League of Nations on coercion.* What was a mad project for the American states in 1787 is a far madder project for the European states in 1937. "It is a dream. It is impossible."

But for those who would embark the League on more profitable forms of co-operation, with a view to reducing the likelihood that these nations will "want to fight," the difficulties are less. Forms of international co-operation, and the means for achieving it, unknown and undreamed of in 1787, are now awaiting a statesmanship wise enough to make the most of them. It will be a tragedy if they are neglected, and the attempt made to restore the principle of coercion into a League of sovereign states each armed and still arming in the determination not to be coerced in any form or from any source. National sovereignty and collective coercion cannot co-exist. If either is to stand the other must go. Which is it to be?

Were it possible to summon Alexander

Hamilton to a general council for the reform of the Covenant we cannot doubt what line he would take. He would urge the total elimination of the coercive element as the first step to further progress. To which we add, on our own account, that if that were done, the chief obstacle would be removed which has hitherto kept the United States out of the League. Were there no other argument for eliminating coercion, this should be enough.

Augsburg Seminary
Library